RITUAL BODY ART

RITUAL BODY ART
DRAWING THE SPIRIT

CHARLES ARNOLD

Phoenix Publishing Inc.

This edition printed 1997

PHOENIX PUBLISHING, INC.
Portal Way
P.O. Box 10
Custer, Washington USA 98240

Distributed in Canada by
PHOENIX PUBLISHING INC.
821 - 254th Street
Langley, BC V4W 2R8

ISBN 0-919345-74-3

Cover photograph: Sam Short
Cover design: Creative Circus
Editor: Diane Conn Darling
Production: L. Brown and M. Shutty

Printed in Hong Kong

Contents

Acknowledgments 6
Foreword 7
1   Introduction to Body Art 9
2   A Brief History of Body Decoration 15
3   How Body Art Works Its Magic 23
4   Some Symbols Used in Body Art 30
5   Meanings of the Colors 57
6   Ritual and Makeup 66
7   Masks and Masking 72
8   Ritual Apparel and Props 83
9   Ritual Jewelry 88
10 Scents 98
11 The Setting for Ritual Body Art 118
12 Full Body Art 130
13 Sabbats, Esbats and the Elements 146
14 Everyday Use of Ritual Body Art 152
    Sources 155
    Appendix—Colors of Catal Huyuk 159

Acknowledgments

This book is the product of many year's work and devotion; not only by myself but by my wife, Vykki, to whom I dedicate it. I also dedicate it to my departed friend and teacher, the last person arrested for the crime of Witchcraft in North America, Roy Dymond.

I also wish to thank the many people who, over the years have stood by me when it would have been much easier to do otherwise, especially Ginni Jacques-Martin, Linda Castleton, Carol Jamele, and Sea-Ra.

Thank you one and all, may your lives be filled with joy and bliss and may we all one day meet again and remember...

Foreword

Attend any major outdoor Pagan festival in the summertime, and you will notice an increasing number of people sporting tattoos, from the exquisite and dainty to the elaborate and colorful, some depicting entire mythological scenes and archetypal imagery. Check out the face-painted Lakota in *Dancing With Wolves*, or the woad-painted Highland warriors in *Braveheart*, and recall that the ancient Picts were so-called because of the intricate pictoglyphs adorning their bodies. Flesh-painting has become a fine art much in demand at Pagan festivals. Many artists now ply this trade, producing spectacular full-body decorations for naked bonfire dancers.

According to author Charles Arnold human beings have practiced magical arts including body decoration for more than 20,000 years. These activities are acts of consciousness alteration and communion with the Great Goddess.

Charles is a Wiccan Priest and has studied and practiced the art of ritual body painting and decoration for over 20 years. He has worked with symbols, colors, designs and masks of many traditional Pagan cultures, both ancient and modern, from votive figurines of the pre-Kurgan civilizations of Old Europe to African and Native American tribal body art. Ritual experiments were conducted with students in Charles' Mystical Practices Study Group, along with volunteers from Toronto's Spendweik

‡ ✕ △ ◇ ✳ □ N✕ ✳ ▽ ◈ ᖴ △ 人 ⌐ ⌐ ⊖ ▷ ⊞ ⊼ △

Coven and the Temple of the Elder Faiths, and from the Order of the White Mare of Mississauga, Ontario.

The historical section of the book does a wonderful job of explaining why people decorate themselves and provides archaeological evidence and biblical references. The discussions on how body art works its magic (including the use of theatrical makeup) are applied to rites of passage, sabbats, esbats, and other rituals. Most insightful are the chapters on the meanings of colors, mask making, ritual apparel and props, jewelry (with meaning of various gemstones), scents, and ritual scripts (including samples). By using Charles' methods, any ritual occasion can be turned into a wondrous pageant. As a magician, I particularly valued the many pages of magical and alchemical symbols, runes, glyphs and sigils, with full explanations, which I intend to make great use of.

This book is a grimoire extraordinaire—"a must-have" for any magickal library.

OBERON ZELL
Church of All Worlds
Green Egg magazine

Chapter 1
Introduction to Body Art

For a large part of our history, probably more than twenty thousand years, human beings have practiced a wide variety of magical arts that include decorating their bodies. Such activities were and are acts of worship, consciousness alteration, and identification and communication with the Great Goddess. Body decoration is a form of magic. Since the fall of Goddess-worshipping societies, beginning around the fourth millennium BCE, such practices have been pushed further and further out of favor until they were at last judged to be blasphemous. They were placed outside of the law, along with female leadership in religious celebrations, ritual nudity, and partnership (rather than domination) as the foundation of human relationships. As society "progressed," these practices became targets of persecution and either disappeared or became so alien to the accepted social, moral and spiritual norms, that their use was judged to be heretical. The Western world, based on religious laws contained in the Torah, the Koran and the Bible, now considers these practices to be signs of social and individual decadence and blasphemy.

But blasphemy and decadence were far from the minds of our ancestors when they practiced body decoration in their worship and their lives. Rather, body decoration, as demonstrated by their statuary, was a means of identification with the Goddess and the forces of nature and life, perhaps in an effort to communicate a living prayer to Her. Such decoration was used to remind both wearer and observer that human beings are part of, and one of, the forces of nature, rather than set apart from them. Body art was used to bring about personal empowerment, to celebrate various rites of passage, to heal the body and the mind, and to generally alter reality to bring it more closely in accordance with the will—in other words, to make magic.

Body decorations were probably used privately for any number of personal reasons, but such art was more often a part of the community's social and spiritual rituals: magics of the Earth and the sky, of the field and the furrow and the hunt, and of all the creatures of the Goddess. These rites drew people into closer harmony with one another and with the force of life and its celebration, rather than with the forces of domination and destruction.

Today, despite the changes that have taken place since those early times, and despite the fact that society tries so hard to alienate people one from another, this art form and the magic it holds continues to draw us. Even after millennia it reaches out and speaks to us. We are fascinated by body art we see in such movies as *Dances With Wolves*, *The Emerald Forest* or *Quest for Fire*. Museum exhibits, art shows and theatrical presentations that feature dramatic changes to personal appearance attract us. Even costume parties and Halloween are taken as opportunities to reawaken that primitive but balanced person.

But does body art and costuming still contain the power to heal and empower? For those who take the time to learn them and work with them respectfully, and who manage to overcome their socially-induced fears of life, beauty and the personal experience of the Goddess, the answer is a resounding "Yes."

My Search

My first introduction to ritual body decoration occurred more than twenty years ago. At that time I was studying with a member of the Kiowa men's Dog Society who was also a member of the

Native American Movement, an activist deeply involved with the Native American cultural renaissance of the late 1960s and early 1970s. He introduced me to the uses of color, symbol and visage as practiced by his people for generations. This strong, wise man was the first person to show me the power there.

A decade later I began investigating the spiritual and cultural roots of my newly-adopted religion, Wicca, as well as other Pagan religions. This, in turn, led to an interest in the archaeology and anthropology of the earliest Goddess-worshipping peoples and places, the pre-Kurgan civilizations of Central and Southeastern Europe. I quickly became fascinated by some of the objects that had been discovered: figurines with their faces covered by masks and their bodies exhibiting a variety of symbols and colors. I began to notice that certain symbols and masks occurred on specific types of figures. Additional research showed that a great many of these symbols and ones very similar to them were used by "primitive" cultures around the world. Finally, by reading Marija Gimbutas's, *The Language of the Goddess*, I saw that not only do such symbols constitute the first written language, but that comparable languages are alive in the world today.

I continued reading the works of researchers and investigators such as Edwin O. James, Jacquetta Hawkes, Joseph Campbell, Olivia Vlahos, Michel Thevoz, Clarence Turner, James Mellaart, and Marilyn and Anthony Strathern. All reinforced my impression that body art and masking were valid and central elements in the worship rituals of various "primitive" peoples. I began to believe that these practices, common to all the most ancient peoples of Old Europe, might be brought back to life.

I noted that votive statues of the Goddesses and Gods of these peoples, as well as the walls of their temples and perhaps even their homes, were covered with designs and symbols. Many of these were colored or displayed evidence of previous coloring, which served to strengthen my idea as well as offer examples of the masks, symbols and colors that might be used. Gimbutas's work, along with Riane Eisler's, *The Chalice and the Blade*, provided additional reinforcement and expanded my understanding of the development and use of the symbolic written languages by the "Old Society" of ancient Europe.

Equally interesting was the link between body art and masking, evidenced by the large number of these votive figures representing the Goddess or Her priestesses wearing masks. Support for this link is the central role masking continues to play in various Earth religions, such as that of the Hopi and Zuni.

Much of my initial research was in the area of permanent body decoration as practiced in primitive societies. This is divided into three categories. Tattooing is the permanent coloring of parts of the body through injection of a dye beneath the skin. Cicatrization, instead of using a dye, calls for the injection of a sterile but irritating substance such as wood ash, causing scars to form below the surface and resulting in superficial bumps and ridges. Scarification is the continued cutting and irritation of the skin to form large scars at the surface. However, I found myself drawn to the concept of temporary body art as it had been and, in certain societies, continues to be practiced. Everything I read or saw during this time reinforced my conviction that such mystical art can and should be used once again as a powerful magical tool in the quest for Goddess and partnership consciousness. Such religious art could not only be a powerful adjunct to various rites of passage and other celebratory and mystical rites and rituals, but it could also be a strongly religious experience in and of itself.

I began to draw more from archeological and anthropological sources as I became increasingly certain that certain subjective phenomena could be recreated; phenomena which drew on subconscious archetypes little influenced by the passage of time. The votive statues of Catal Huyuk, Hacilar and Ras Shamra; frescoes of Knossos; the cave paintings of Lascaux, Les Trois Freres and Font de Gaume—all of these served to strengthen my intuitive knowledge that I was on the track of something truly wonderful. They also supplied me with dozens, hundreds, of additional symbols and color symbolisms, all of which I began to use in my work.

Hands-On Research

It was at this juncture that I came to understand that reading the research of others would not be enough. I would either have to attempt the resuscitation of this art form myself, or write my research for publication as just another sterile article. This book is evidence that I chose the former course of action. Personal and group experimentation has allowed me to prove that the magic of prehistoric peoples who lived 20,000 to 30,000 years ago can be re-created.

Students in my Mystical Practices Study Group, along with volunteers from three Pagan groups—Spendweik Coven and the Temple of the Elder Faiths, both of Toronto, and The Order of the White Mare of Mississauga, Ontario—served as my early canvasses, as it were. They were invited to participate in my experiments and to note their subjective reactions to the applications of the symbols and colors. To put it mildly, their reactions were exciting for all of us. Several expressed the feeling that they could sense their personalities changing as the colors were applied. They felt power raining down or flowing up into them from the Earth. They even noted an increase in attributes such as strength and stability as the symbol began to be applied, even when they didn't know what the symbol meant. Eventually many of them chose to use body art as an intrinsic part of their meditation or worship practices.

Seeing these results but seeking additional input, I began to give workshops on temporary body art at Pagan festivals across Canada and the United States. People at Rites of Spring, Pan-Pagan Festival, Wic-Can Fest and Goddess Gathering who attended these workshops volunteered to be painted. Again, they could feel the magic happen to them.

Body Art Practice

Today I work with a number of apprentices, individual students and groups across North America, sharing the knowledge we have gained and experimenting further with the techniques we have developed. Using sacred designs and a color system based on that of Neolithic and Paleolithic Europe (along with some later additions), and masking techniques of both ancient and contemporary "primitive peoples," we have been able to achieve results that can only be described as remarkable for the subjects, the artists, and for those who participate in the rituals where our art is used.

In her book *Body, The Ultimate Symbol*, Olivia Vlahos writes,

> Paint binds and separates, defining the pairs of opposites: sacred-profane, male-female, sick-well, good-bad, high-low, living-dead. Paint sets human beings apart from nature, while at the same time putting them in touch with natural forces apprehended but dimly understood. Paint announces the crisis times of life and announces them on the bodies of individuals in stress. By the power and meaning of color, feelings are channeled and vulnerability protected. By color are companions notified to give support and consolation. In paint a community displays collective values and sustains social commitment. By looking much like everyone else, the individual demonstrates participation and belief in a common identity. Finally, paint communicates on the outer skin something of the inner self. It is a self enlargement, idealized, enhanced. And the soul rejoices and is content. *Paint me as I long to be and need to be and am.* This is the message of the graphic body. *Paint me brave. Paint me charming. Paint me clever, able, wise. Paint me eager to please but to mine own self true. Paint me human.*

Chapter 2
A Brief History of Body Decoration

In order to fully understand body art it is necessary to understand the reasons behind body decoration. By learning the answers to questions such as "How long ago did the practice begin?" and "How widespread was the practice?" we may gain a more complete understanding of the subject as a whole. If we follow by answering such questions as "Which of these practices are still being followed?" and "In what sociological context is this done?" we will emerge with new insight, not only into the practice of body decoration, but into the power of magic to change our own lives and surroundings.

Personal Decoration

Modern use of personal decoration varies widely. It can be seen in the three-piece, razor stripe, navy blue wool suit which indicates "power and money elite," just as clearly as in the "colors" of various gang members. It ranges from the uniforms of military and para-military personnel to the tattoos former prison inmates wear to indicate to those who understand the meanings of the symbols, where they were imprisoned, what crime they were imprisoned for, and even to which groups in prison they belonged. In short, it is one of the strongest indicators of status within society, both for the over-culture and the underculture.

Anthropologists tell us that there are several basic reasons why people decorate themselves. One of the most important is for display: the use of decoration to draw attention to a person as a whole or to some particular characteristic(s) that he/she may possess. These characteristics may include strength, wealth, courage, fertility or some other feature that is viewed positively by the society. Decoration for display is used to impress others, as immediately after coming of age, during courtship or when seeking to gather followers.

Body art is also used as a form of self-suggestion in helping to change habits, or in healings, and may be considered a type of applied visualization or a self-triggering device. Personal decoration was and is also used to indicate the status of a particular individual with regard to a specific social function. Among the Plains nations of North America, red stripes applied around the eyes of women indicated that they had been captured and taken as wives in the last bride kidnapping games.

Body decoration is a means of group identification by the application of specific cultural symbols or colors common to all members of a society. For example, in the Crow Nation the use of red and yellow on the face of a man was reserved for members of the Big Dog Society, a warrior and service group. Other examples are rites of passage, such as First Blood Ritual, where the young woman is decorated as part of the initiatory process involving a group, in this case, the society of mature women. First blood symbology varies, but is generally reflective of change and availability as a mate.

Body art is also used for disguise. The simplest type would be camouflage, the coloring of the face and body in order to make them more difficult to detect against a background, used in hunting and warfare. Another disguise used in "primitive" warfare is the disguising of the face so that one's enemies, or the enemies' gods or spirits, will not know the identity of the person engaged in combat against them. Often this is also a type of group identification, designed to show the enemy that they are attacked or opposed by a specific people, but hiding the personal identities of the individuals representing that group. The warriors of the Mt. Hagen society of New Zealand, before adding colors, first cover their faces with black, thus rendering themselves invisible to the spirits of dead warriors of other tribes.

Another reason for body decoration is for self-transformation. This is shamanic or magical body art, designed to change the person upon whom the pigments and symbols are applied. The great majority of examples contained in this book are of self-transformational art. Traditionally, self-transformational art is applied in a ritual context, for example, in a sacred setting or space, using colors and other materials that have been created and set aside specifically for such use. In many cultures the symbols applied represent the guardian animals or spirits of the person being decorated. In others, the colors and designs follow tradition. In nearly all cases, each individual is allowed to alter the colors and designs to some degree so as to make them more personally powerful.

Body decoration is also used to increase personal power, calling upon the assistance of a guardian animal or spirit. Many of these symbols are the tribal or power symbols of the user's particular culture. Power art appears similar to display art, but the intent is completely different. Display art shows the power of the wearer, while power art is, in effect, a prayer to a higher force. Healers use this style of body art to draw power into themselves so that they can use it to heal others. Like self-transformational art, power art is usually applied in a ritual setting.

Humans also practice body decoration for protection; such decorations are often combined with power designs. The power is directed inward, so as to push the energy outward. In protection the focus is outward, toward guardian spirits and gods, calling on those energies to protect an individual whose essential focus, no matter what the activity, is inward. This type of art is often applied to those who require healing. Protection art is regularly applied in both ritual and non-ritual settings.

Thus we see that human cultures use color and symbol as magical tools to communicate with the forces of nature, alter their consciousness, bring about personal empowerment, celebrate various rites of passage, heal themselves and others, and generally alter reality to bring it more closely in accordance with their will. Body decoration is a personal magic that may be applied by the subject, or it may require the assistance of friends or a human spiritual guide. What it most emphatically does not require is an intermediary between the individual and his gods or spirits.

Biblical References

Though permanent body decorations as mentioned above (tattooing, cicatrization and scarification) are probably later forms, they are more adequately documented than are practices of temporary body decoration. The *Old Testament* refers to tattooing at least once and scarification three times, all apparently in connection with mourning rites for the dead. In Leviticus 19:28, we read, "Ye shall not make any cuttings in your flesh for the dead, nor print any marks upon you"; and in 21:5, "They shall not make baldness upon their head, neither shall they shave off the corner of their beard, nor make any cuttings in their flesh." Another reference to scarification occurs in Deuteronomy 14:1, "Ye are the children of the Lord your God: ye shall not cut yourselves, nor make any baldness between your eyes for the dead." Opposition to body art is based on another *Old Testament* verse, Genesis 1:27, "So God created man in His own image, in the image of God created He him; male and female created He them."

However, in the *New Testament* book of Revelations we find

several references, both positive and negative, to tattoos or "marks" applied to the followers of Christ and the followers of the anti-Christ. The first of these occurs in Revelations 7:3, "Hurt not the earth, neither the sea, not the trees, till we have sealed the servants of our God in their foreheads." This concept of marking the foreheads of the "saved" continues through five additional verses. In Revelations 13:16-17, we again see references made to marks on the body, this time of a negative nature: "And he causeth all, both small and great, rich and poor, free and bond, to receive a mark in their right hand, or in their foreheads. And that no man might buy or sell, save he that had the mark, or the name of the beast, or the number of his name." References, both positive and negative, continue throughout the book. Another positive reference is found in Galatians 6:17: "In the future let no one make trouble for me for I bear the mark of Jesus branded on my body." (New Standard Edition)

Prohibitions against marking the body with tattoos also appear in the Koran. Still, there is a long tradition of tattooing among the majority of Moslem peoples around the world. The contradiction that this situation seems to present is readily solved, at least for many, by the belief that the soul will be purified by fire prior to entering Paradise. This divine fire will cleanse the body as well, removing any forbidden marks.

This is very close to the beliefs of a number of Christian sects that teach that the body is the Temple of Christ and, as such, should not be defiled in any way, especially tattooing, which is considered blasphemous. The argument in defense of tattooing states that all those who rise on judgement day shall do so in perfection, without decay and, obviously, without their offending tattoos.

Archaeological Evidence

Older evidence of body decoration includes four Egyptian

mummies that date from the 11th Dynasty or second millennium BCE. Oddly, all were women, three evidently from Thebes, while the other was from Nubia. All were marked with rows of blue-black dots on the arms and legs as well as on the lower abdomen, where the common design was the lozenge, an ancient fertility symbol.

In *Body, The Ultimate Symbol*, Olivia Vlahos discusses even older body decoration. She examines the research of the noted French archaeologist Francois Bordes. In his findings, Bordes makes reference to "crayons" or lumps of ocher and manganese oxides, some of which had been rubbed, indicating that the pigment may have been applied directly to the skins of these ancient people. This conclusion is reached because other, similar lumps, had been scratched in a way that indicated that the scratches were produced in an effort to remove some of the powder for other uses. The amazing point about Bordes's work is that his research was conducted in Neanderthal sites, dating from approximately 70,000 years ago. Evidence also indicates that these early proto-humans practiced coloring the bodies of their dead with red ocher or, as was sometimes done, buried bodies in round pits surrounded by this red stone. Vlahos estimates that the practice of body painting goes back as far as four hundred thousand years.

Later evidence, this time from Homo Sapien, is found in cave paintings at Lascaux and many other Paleolithic sites in France and Spain. These paintings feature decorated bodies and date from before 5,000 BCE.

In the first centuries before and after the beginning of the Common Era, warriors from various Celtic tribes applied wode, a blue herbal dye, to their bodies before a battle. A mixture of wode and limestone paste produced shades of green. Several early sources refer to tattooing by the Celts as well. The historian Tertullian decried the practice of North African women who tattooed themselves and one another, calling these designs *Stigmata Britonum*, or British marks. In later times this prejudice became so overwhelming that the Northumbrian Synod of Calcuth (787 CE) forbade all forms of tattooing and body decoration because of their obviously Pagan roots.

In a slightly earlier time frame we find numerous Greek and Roman writers describing markings common among the Scythians, Dacians and Thracians. These were permanent in nature, being a combination of scarification and tattooing. The general opinion of the "civilized" Greeks was that the custom was vulgar and disgusting because it was practiced by peoples they considered to be barbarians. Even though the Greeks were Pagan, nearly all of them exhibited a clear prejudice against these customs. Their attitudes were amazingly similar to later Christian and Moslem views, although for cultural rather than religious reasons.

Modern Ritual Body Art

A vast amount of evidence worldwide reflects extensive use of cicatrization and scarification, along with the application of colored oils. The Nuba and other body art we see in Africa today is but a remnant of a practice which for thousands of years covered nearly the entire continent. In various parts of India we still find symbolic tattooing that dates back at least two to three thousand years.

Native North Americans have used temporary body art as part of their social and spiritual lives for hundreds of generations. It has been used to a greater or lesser extent by members of nearly every nation across the continent. During the conscious and unconscious period of caricaturization of Native Americans by Euro-American settlers, this spiritual and social practice was demeaned. Denied its spiritual context, such marks eventually became a couple of streaks of whatever happened to be handy, applied to let everyone know that the person wearing it was "on the war path."

Fortunately, a few spiritually aware individuals remained deeply rooted in their cultures and their communities. They passed on their knowledge of the true meanings of such personal art in the history of their peoples. In a number of instances, artists, historians, and social scientists such as Ruth Bunzel, George Caitlin, Edward Curtis and Edwin Denig, have recorded these practices in an accurate historical context. Thus, we are seeing a revival of body art among Native peoples in the spiritual and social realms of their lives.

Even more interesting as a culture is the Mt. Hageners of New Zealand, where the great majority of the people practiced body decoration until quite recently and where it is still used for special occasions today. Among such groups one can still learn from the practitioners, in their own words, the reasons for which body art was first practiced; the reasons why, despite all obstacles, it has survived; and the reasons for its renaissance.

Chapter 3
How Body Art Works Its Magic

The application of color, archetypal symbols, masks and ritual clothing and jewelry, among other techniques, opens pathways between the conscious mind and the subconscious. Anyone involved with acting and the theater who has experienced the transformation that takes place during the makeup process, has shared this experience. But the reasons for this amazing change are not completely understood and are interpreted differently by nearly all who have experienced it.

In a ritual context, it is often thought that the objects, symbols and colors have a magical quality in and of themselves, holding or creating the energy necessary to accomplish the desired results directly. I tend to share this view, based on my own experience and on years of scientific research into the effects of color on the personality and the ability of symbols to affect the subconscious. I believe that the response to the process has been indelibly etched on the individual and collective subconscious. When symbols are applied in an appropriate context, it triggers a part of the primal human memory and opens a doorway between the conscious and subconscious long used by our ancestors but left closed for generations. Once this process begins, it acts to free ancient memories and energies that reside within, or are created by, the body and mind of each individual.

There are those who choose not to bother themselves with long and involved explanations, preferring instead to say that the process brings them closer to their Muse and, as such, in harmony with the Universal Will. Such a philosophy suggests that any action, performed in harmony with a Universal Will or Divine Energy, must be successful because it is the intent of that Force or Will. Nothing in these two seemingly divergent points of view is contradictory; one speaks to the mind while the other addresses the soul. Because of this compound view, once the process begins, individual initiative, tempered only by training, self-discipline and divine inspiration, must be allowed free rein.

Rites and Symbols

When I first began my investigation and sharing my knowledge with others, I was working under what I later decided was a false premise: that the primary interests of the "primitive" peoples, whose symbols I saw and used, centered on physical strength, fertility and attraction. I assumed that these people's strongest symbols and most powerful rituals would center on these topics because the symbols and rituals were close to the heart of their survival. So I began my early art and my first workshops with a focus on these areas. Later investigations led me to broaden my view of the peoples and societies of Old Europe and their religious lives and practices.

I started to research the next obvious ritual area, rites of passage, as generally practiced around the world and as most likely practiced in Old European society. Such rites may have played a major role in the spiritual life of Old Europeans. It was my belief that similar rites, whether they are adopted from currently extant cultures, re-created from history or myth, or simply created anew, could play a central healing role in our own culture.

It is unfortunate that so little emphasis is placed on formal rites of passage, especially among young males. In recent years Paganism has done so much to revive or re-create some such rituals. However, much of the emphasis has been on rituals for women. Rites of passage for boys would go far in helping men feel more secure in themselves. This would serve to decrease the level of violence in society brought about by young men seeking ways to prove their manhood. It is a shame that nearly the only place in which such rituals currently take place is in the street gang, and where they are the focus of much attention and energy.

The First Designs

Beginning with the First Blood Ritual, which focuses on menarche or female coming of age, I set about creating a piece of body art that would reflect the physical and social reality that such a rite would embody and, at the same time, serve as a ritual educational vehicle. My first work was with a 12 year-old female Pagan from Florida who, along with her parents, attended a workshop on body art that I gave at the Pan-Pagan Festival in 1984. This young woman had not yet reached menarche, but was expecting onset quite soon. I worked with her for several hours, painting, asking her to express what she was feeling, and asking her mother for input as well. All the time I applied the design, we continued to talk.

I began with a green inverted triangle on her abdomen, then outlined it in red, reminding her that the green indicated her soon-to-be-realized fertility. Outlining this triangle in red, we discussed how that fertility was wrapped in the blood that would soon flow. Then, starting at the top of her head, I painted a red vertical line to the red triangle outline on her abdomen, explaining that this represented her bloodline, her line of descent. (This pattern is illustrated in the picture section and described in Chapter 12.)

Interactive work like this helped me refine my technique, the collection of symbols used, and the explanation I create to accompany the painting process. This particular design is now widely accepted and generally used across North America with only minor personal modifications.

Of course my next project was the creation of a design for a young man undergoing his own coming of age ritual. Because of the emotional ambiguity attached to this type of ritual due to the infrequency of it practice, this pattern took quite a long time to come together. But a strong, simple design eventually came into being and soon designs for other rites of passage came into existence: for conception, for each of the three trimester rituals and for birthing; designs for handfasting and handparting, for croning (menopause), and for death. Other magics came, too, either on their own or at the request of someone who thought that an application of particular body symbols might help them. There is art that helps mend a broken bone or banish a migraine, designs created to attract a lover or aid in meditation or concentration, and even patterns designed to help develop a new skill or ability.

Tools and Materials

In addition to the power of the symbols and the colors, I came to realize that there could be power in the tools and materials themselves. My basic ritual or magical pigments are the red of red ocher, the white of kaolin clay or wood ash, and the black of manganese dioxide or ground charcoal. These pigments and colors have been used for more than 300 centuries—the colors of power, the focus of mystical belief for more than 1,200 generations. With only these three colors, all emotions, all desires, all the stages of life and forces of nature can be expressed.

However, in order to create subtle magics and to affect people with colors with which they can relate comfortably, I supple-

ment these basic pigments with other shades of ocher to pro-
duce yellows, oranges and browns, sometimes umbers, and I
use wode or finely ground blue corn for shades of blue. For
green, I combine powdered limestone with wode, following
the ancient Celtic methods. These pigments are added to an
organic medium, usually a lanolin cream or animal tallow, to
provide a non-hardening, body-insulating coloration that may
even be beneficial for the skin.

For some rituals I have a variety of clays (kaolin, terra cotta,
etc.) in a powder form, just as they are dug from the earth,
sometimes mixed with water and applied as a paste. Though
after as little as half an hour, such clay-based pastes dry and
crack, sometimes painfully. However, they feel right for some
specific uses. The secret to prevent complete hardening is to
add about a teaspoon of dish detergent to each pint of coloring.

Some other points about using raw clays: they tend to dry the
skin very badly, so if you use them, after washing be sure to
apply oil over your wet skin or use a moisturizing cream.
However, in the process of drying, clay also tends to draw
toxins and impurities out of the skin, leaving it much cleaner
on the deeper levels.

For demonstration purposes I depend on non-toxic acrylic
colors and water color concentrates. I have learned to take the
time and care to ensure that my subjects have no allergic
reactions to pigment or medium. I begin by asking them if they
know of any allergies and, if they are uncertain, I apply a small
dab of color, magical or demonstrative, to their back or to the
inside of their arm and wait 10 to 15 minutes. If there is
swelling, inflammation, itchiness, or if they feel a tightening
of the chest, swelling of the eyes or other symptom, I immediately cleanse the area and advise them to see their doctor. I use
these modern materials not because they have no power, for
they most certainly do, but because they are easier to apply
and remove and they take less time to prepare.

Another tool that I have begun to use in conjunction with my

work is aroma. If, for example, I know that I will be creating a design with a particular focus, I will take the time to mix various appropriate essential oils with my pigments, utilizing those that will supplement and reinforce my desired end result.

For most work I use good quality brushes, usually of pig bristle or squirrel or ermine hair. I have found that good brushes, properly kept, far outlast cheap brushes. For those times when I apply pigments in a more primitive manner or using materials such as fat-based pigments or raw clays, the best results are achieved by applying them by hand. However, a point that must be remembered here is that what you are doing is quite intimate. When done by hand, it might make your subject uncomfortable and your work ineffectual. For such situations, a brush can be created by cutting a small twig of oak, sassafras, or willow, and chewing the end in order to split the fibers, in the same manner as has been done for thousands of years.

When using dry pigments, one ancient way of applying color is to blow the pigment onto the body using a straw. Blow through the straw, across the palate where the dry pigments are held, and onto the body. This is usually done to cover large areas. Where some areas are not to be painted, they are covered by the subject's hand or some other item. This technique is very ancient, being found in many neolithic cave paintings.

I believe in what I'm doing and have faith in my results. To use inferior quality materials or tools would only weaken my power and the power of the symbols, colors and scents that I apply. For the same reason I prefer to use the more ancient symbols, pigments and techniques, firm in the belief that these will bring about a stronger response from our deeper shared memories.

Other Applications

One additional point: for those adept at visualization and similar techniques, the information contained in this book, the symbols, the colors and the rest, can all be used as aids in your work. There is no requirement that you apply brush to pigment, then to body, if you can visualize effectively. Likewise, for those who work with poppet or candle magic, the colors and symbols contained here will also prove to make your work more efficient and effective. But please realize that these are powerful tools, revered by many peoples. They are given in order to help you grow and empower yourself and to help others, not to expose the mystical practices of "primitive" peoples to scorn. I ask that you, in your work, revere the beliefs of the peoples from whom we have learned so much.

Chapter 4
Some Symbols Used in Body Art

The many symbols that you can use in ritual makeup or body art come from a myriad of sources: Neolithic and Paleolithic cave paintings, various runic alphabets, hieroglyphics, traditional magical symbols, and even folk symbols from around the world. The sources section will supply you with a number of references for your own research. Keep in mind that the symbols that are the strongest for you are those that give rise to the strongest feeling in you, so don't be afraid to cautiously experiment even if it contradicts some of the meanings given here.

(To) Accomplish.

This is a traditional folk symbol. The vertical line indicates the desired goal. The wedge represents the individual's desire to go beyond that goal.

Air.

These are three symbols for Air. The first two are derived from alchemy, while the third is loosely based on astrology.

Attraction.

This is an extremely old symbol, dating back to the Paleolithic era, and has several meanings, of which Attraction is the first.

Boy.

This is based on the astrological symbol for Man. The wedge is left off of the shaft to illustrate the lack of adulthood.

Change.

This is another traditional symbol from folklore, very similar to the symbol for to Accomplish. The feet at the ends of the wedge indicate that the event is real and will soon or already has taken place.

Child, Unborn.

The first symbol is the circle. An alternative, the second symbol, is really an enlarged indicator of Pregnancy. Both are derived from folklore.

Childbirth.

Because of the importance of childbirth there are a number of symbols for the event. The first is based on a Paleolithic design, the second a philosophical symbol, and the rest are

derived from folklore. The fourth symbol indicates the feet above the earth, or "alive."

Children.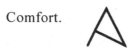

The first of these symbols is the same as for Unborn Child, but with the dot in the center demonstrating independent life. The second and third are the symbols for Girl and Boy, and the final symbol is the Rune "Beorc," an indicator of child or children.

Comfort.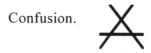

The roots of this symbol are unknown. However, indications point to the original meaning as a tent or shelter with the doorway open, indicating hospitality.

Constraint.

The first symbol is derived from folklore and seems to indicate that the individual (the vertical line) is restrained, not once, but thrice, the number of power. The latter three are variations on the Rune "Nied."

Confusion.

This is possibly a philosophical or demonstrative symbol. Based on the triangle as representing Order, the broken triangle would have the opposite meaning.

Counter.

The origin of this folk symbol is not known. It has long been used to represent an opposing force.

Counterspell.

This sigil is based on Counter. The added line demonstrates that the individual is working on two levels, the physical and the magickal.

Daughter.

Like the symbol for boy, this is an incomplete astrological symbol.

Death.

Derived from folklore. The opposite of birth, this time the individual is below the ground, thus dead or buried.

Defense.

The basis for the first symbol is obvious: a line of spears or pointed sticks joined together to create a defensive barrier. The second symbol indicates the need for defense in all directions. The third symbol is the traditional defense Rune, "Yr."

Desire, Sexual.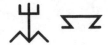

The first symbol is the same Neolithic design as is used for Childbirth, but here representing a woman in a sexually receptive position. The second, a folk symbol, is a slightly simplified and stylized version of the same thing.

Disaster.

This symbol is the Rune "Ear," and represents destruction by the forces of nature.

Disrupt a Relationship.

This is a simple combination of the symbols for Woman and Man, barred from one another.

Disruption.

The first of these symbols is philosophical in nature, the lines disrupting the simplicity and unity of the circle. The second is from folklore, the exact symbolism of which is unknown. The remainder are variants of "Hagall," the Rune for disruption.

Dream.

This shows an individual with the wavy world of unreality over its head.

Earth.

The first two symbols are derived from alchemy. The third is astrological in origin.

Enemies, Female.

This symbol represents two women at odds, indicated by the aggressive angles that they take toward one another.

Enemies, Male.

This is the same theme as for female enemies.

Energy, sending.

This very useful symbol is the Rune "Gar."

Enthusiasm.

This Rune, "Tyr," symbolizes enthusiasm. In the extreme it also denotes the berserker.

Family.

The first symbol is from folklore. It shows a woman, a man and two children. The second is the combination of the astrological symbols for Woman and Man. For alternative families, this sigil can be altered to represent any arrangement.

Fear.

The first of these symbols shows the individual being attacked from all sides, causing fear. The second is an Egyptian hieroglyph.

Femaleness.

The first is Neolithic, and represents the vulva, while the second and third are much later and show different phases of the moon as a symbol for femaleness. The fourth symbol is a vague outline of the abdomen, indicating the seat of fertility.

Fertility, Animal.

The first is the plowed and seeded field, a Neolithic design

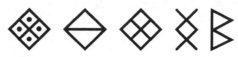

indicating fertility of all types. The second is a variant of the Rune "Ing," and the third is one variant of the Rune "Beorc."

Fertility, Human.

The first, fourth and fifth are the same symbols as used to represent animal fertility. The second symbol is a lozenge, the generic shape for fertility, with a horizontal line representing that which travels over the earth. The third symbol is the plowed field, the lozenge divided on the diagonal in a manner similar to the first symbol.

Fertility, Plant.

These are the same symbols as for animal and human Fertility, with the difference that there is a vertical line in the lozenge, indicating those things which grow up out of the earth.

Fight.

Little is known about how this symbol obtained this meaning. One conjecture is that the vertical and horizontal lines portray the spirit between two people, with the horizontal line illustrating acceptable behavior. The change to unacceptable behavior leading to confrontation.

Fire.

Alchemical and astrological signs. Another astrological meaning for the second symbol is the Sun.

Flow.

This is the principal symbol used to denote flow of either materials or emotions.

Flow, Decrease.

The meaning of this folk symbol is completely obvious when read from below.

Flow, Increase.

The reverse of the symbol above. Here the concept is time: first one drop, then two, then many.

Foe, Insurmountable.

This rarely used symbol is the Rune "Ior." It may be applied to make the subject impossible to defeat in some venture.

Friends, Female.

This symbol represents two women, close together, obviously friends.

Friends, Male.

The same as above, but using male symbols.

Future.

The basic symbol is the combination of vertical and horizontal lines. In this symbol, time is completely fluid and the specific meaning is only understood by the horizontal line, which indicates the future.

Gain.

This is the Rune "Othel," which also means inheritances, property and, to a lesser degree, added responsibilities.

Girl.

The astrological symbol for Venus and, thus, Woman. The figure is incomplete illustrating lack of maturity.

Growth.

"Beorc," the Birch Tree Rune, stands for growth because of the fast rate of growth demonstrated by that tree.

Happiness.

Once again, intent must be supreme: the symbol for Happiness is the same as for Comfort. While the two qualities are similar, there are differences, so the artist and the subject must focus on exactly what they want to achieve.

Harvest.

All of these are variations on the Rune, "Jara." The second of the symbols is also very similar to "Ing," the Rune for completion.

Healing.

This symbol represents a person with wholeness or completeness within them.

Home.

Let your imagination wander a little: see yourself asleep under a roof and you can understand the first symbol. The second is even more apparent.

‡⟊△◇✶□N⟊✳▽❖Ᏸ△⅄Γ𐊕ⲐÞ⧻⚚△

Honor.

The Rune "Tyr," one of three Norse gods of war, and of several noble attributes. To completely understand the varied meanings of this Rune you should read about the God the Rune is named for.

Husband.

The first of these symbols is an old tinker or Gypsy symbol representing the top hat of a gentleman. The second is the astrological symbol for Mars or Man, within a circle.

Influence.

This Icelandic Rune (not an alphabetic Rune) represents one person with many hands or with many persons to serve them, thus portraying a very powerful and influential person.

Initiation.

The first symbol, the circle, represents the necklace which, in turn, represents Initiation. The pentagram shows the out-stretched body, offered to the Gods as a sacrifice, one of the true inner meanings of Initiation.

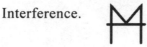

Interference.

This is another symbol that has a meaning attached but no clear history. It has been used by various groups for at least a hundred years and probably much longer.

Intuition.

This is the Rune, "Peorth," along with its variants. Scholars think that this was originally a symbol for a divination game using bones similar to dice, thrown from a cup. This symbol represents the tilted cup.

Invocation, Goddess.

This symbol represents the power of the moon being drawn downward, filling the subject.

Invocation, God.

The same as the preceding, but this time the power is of the sun.

Joy.

The Rune "Wynn."

Learning.

The first of these, a symbol needful of clear intent if it is not to be mistaken for a male triangle, stands for learning and wisdom. Next comes the Rune "Tyr," followed by several variants of the Rune "Ansur."

Love.

The first symbol, the heart, is obvious. The second is the symbol for Family. The addition of a tying line across the family brings it together to show the place of love in the family.

Maleness.

The vertical line is the person. The upright horizontal is the symbol for Potency, thus a masculine symbol.

Man.

The first and third symbols, both anatomical, are Paleolithic, while the second is traditional in folklore. The fourth is a tinker symbol, and is obvious. Next come two traditional symbols, the astrological symbol for Mars and the male version of a triangle. Finally, the last four symbols are all variants of the Rune "Man."

Marriage.

The first of these symbols is the equal combination of male and female triangles, while the second is a Nordic symbol combining the two swastikas, male and female. The third represents two triangles merging, signifying the joining of male and female. They are bound within the circle of love, thus marriage.

More.

These don't really stand for an item, but for the reinforcement of an item. Both are often used in fertility and pregnancy art, placed on or above the breasts, to ensure an adequate supply of milk for nursing.

Movement.

These are variants of the Rune "Eoh," which originally represented a horse.

Obstacle.

This is an old folk symbol, a rather accurate drawing of a well-constructed wall. Sharpened stakes form a vertical wall and are crossed by the two diagonals.

Offering.

The original meaning of the first symbol, an Egyptian hiero-glyph, has been lost. The second, a Rune, seems to indicate merely the location of the offering.

Order.

Coming out of magickal script is this clear, linear, and very male concept of Order.

Overcoming.

This often-used sigil is the Rune "Cweorp."

Partnership.

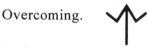

The meaning here is similar to Offering. This Rune, and its variant represent an offer to a partner.

Passage.

This symbol is frequently used, and has a wide variety of applications.

Past.

There is no symbol for time as an object. In this case, three horizontal lines indicate a time that has gone by, the past.

Peace.

This is really a modern symbol. Perhaps that is why the meaning is so clear: the heart of Love surrounded by the circle of Wholeness.

Perseverance.

The first of these symbols is the spear of will which, with force, pierces the wall of resistance only after repeated attempts. The second symbol has no clear interpretation whatsoever and is used merely out of tradition.

Poison.

There are no clear histories of either of these sigils or explanations for their usage, but each has been used for quite some time.

Practicality.

The Rune "Othel" and its variants. Meanings include working in harmony with the will of the Gods and sailing with the prevailing winds.

Practice Magick.

The symbolism of this sigil must be seen as being very close to its alternative meaning, Marriage. Here the meaning is an individual working together with forces other than human, thus the swastikas going in both directions at once.

Prayer (Supplication).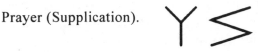

The first symbol shows an individual, arms raised in prayer. The second demonstrates the same thought, kneeling and with head bowed.

Pregnancy.

The first symbol, which is obvious in meaning, is another sigil from folklore while the second is astrological. The other four symbols are Neolithic in origin, one illustrating pregnancy, the others demonstrating the mystery of birth as a maze or fulfilled lozenge.

Present.

Two horizontal bars represent a point halfway between the past and the future.

Protection.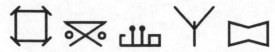

The first of these symbols is traditional and shows a rectangular palisade with corners reinforced to make it stronger. The second symbolizes a strong protector guarding over two children. The third is an Egyptian hieroglyph; I am unaware of the exact symbolism. The fourth is a symbol of a person but, in this context, the action is the arms raised in prayer or invocation, seeking divine protection. The last is the Rune "Stan," representing the shield of Odin, divine protection granted.

Provision.

This ancient symbol represents a bee, provider of honey, the food of the Gods. The bee bestows all good things to the supplicant.

Purification.

I have no idea of the background of this mark. Suffice it to say that it has been used for several centuries and possesses considerable power.

Rebirth.

The first two symbols are variants on the labrys, symbol of the priestesses of the Goddess in ancient time. The symbol does not represent an axe. Rather, it represents a butterfly, a creature that has died and been reborn in a higher state. The third symbol is the Rune "Beorc."

Release of the Soul.

The sigil of Rebirth also indicates Release, as does the second symbol, which represents the soul. When surrounded by a broken circle, it denotes a life which the soul is free to leave.

Repulsion.

The meaning here seems to be quite clear. The vertical line is a barrier that has been attacked. To the right of this is the same arrowhead, this time pushed away, back toward its point of origin.

Retreat.

This symbol is indicative of personal retreat rather than a military manoeuver. The point stands for the soul at the top of the pinnacle, away from the world.

Removal of suffering.

This is a variant of the Rune for joy.

Self.

The vertical line of the person or the circle of the body or relationship make logical representations of Self. The third symbol is the Rune for "Man," one meaning of which is "self" or "me" and is always taken in the first person.

Slander.

This is the same sigil as for Poison. What else is slander but a poisoning of minds and the community toward the person being slandered?

Son.

This is a sigil of unknown origin, which may be taken purely on tradition.

Spirit.

This mark is seen as energy coming from above, as in the invocation sigils.

Stability.

Variations of Runic themes, all of these represent stability of various sorts. The first six are "Ken," followed by four variations of "Ing" and "Ac."

Strength.

The first mark, a very old symbol for Physical Strength, is often painted on the back for strength of body and will. The second is a folk symbol indicating physical strength. It probably originated as a stick drawing of a strong person flexing his or her biceps. Numbers three through five are the Rune "Ur," while the remainder are "Sigel," Runes indicating various types of physical strength.

Strive.

The individual, feet firmly planted on the Earth, still aims high, striving for the stars.

Travel.

The first mark merely shows walking feet. The second, the Rune "Rad," may have been based on this folk symbol.

Union, Sexual.

The first two symbols are just two of hundreds of examples of Neolithic and Paleolithic symbols which may be used for the act of sexual intercourse or conception. The third is a folk sigil made up of the marks for Man and Woman, joined, in a horizontal position. The final mark is the female and male triangles joined.

Unity.

This is similar to the symbol of defense. This time the points are missing from the spears, thus removing the concept of cooperation from the military context.

Unrest.

This is another symbol without a history and, hopefully, one that you will never be called on to use.

Victory.

This symbol is made up of two other symbols, those for Strength and Honor.

Volunteer.

This symbol represents another use for the Rune "Tyr."

Water.

Two symbols, both alchemical in background. Try to envision the latter as a globe or vessel half filled with water.

Wealth.

The first symbol is easy to understand: a man surrounded by piled goods. The next takes a little more concentration, or a better sense of humor: the triangle is a person smoking a pipe. I guess that means that he/she is wealthy enough to take time off to smoke a pipe. The other six are Runes "Feoh" and "Daeg," each with three variations. "Feoh" means wealth in the purest sense (money) while "Daeg" means wealth in the way of goods.

Wholeness.

Our friend the circle makes another appearance, this time as the cycle of existence, everything, shadowed with harmony.

Wife.

This tinker symbol is similar to that for Women. In this case her feet are out, indicating hard work, rather than with the triangle closed to indicate a dress. The second symbol is the astrological Female symbol within the circle of belonging.

Wisdom.

A snake, a nearly universal symbol for wisdom. This sigil can be drawn any way you like, abstract or realistic, in any color, and it still means the same thing. The second symbol is the triangle for learning or knowledge.

Wish.

Similar to the sign for dream, Wish too has a symbol for the non-physical. This time it is below the person, perhaps illustrating the old adage, "Be careful what you wish for, you may get it."

Woman.

These are merely a sample of all the symbols for Woman, second only to the Goddess in the number of symbols with a shared meaning. The first three here are Neolithic and Paleolithic. All represent anatomy, the third indicating pregnancy. The fourth is a tinker sign. Finally, the astrological Venus and the female Triangle of Life.

Magical Alphabets

Should you wish to work with specifics, you may wish to write out your work using a magickal alphabet such as one of those on the chart below. The most commonly used magickal alphabet is Theban (1), of which there are at least five variations, only one of which is included here. Other alphabets are the Runic (2), Enochian (3), Nordic Runes (4), Etruscan (5) and Ogham Script (6). They are arranged so that you can do a straight letter transposition. However, some have letters missing because most earlier alphabets had fewer letters than does ours. For the missing letter "J," substitute the symbol for the letter "I." For "V," substitute the "W."

Modern	(1)	(2)	(3)	(4)	(5)	(6)
A	ꙩ	ᚠ	ꙮ	∩	∧	┼
B	ꙕ	ᛒ	ꙗ	ᚱ		≣
C	Ꙫ		Ꙑ	ᚴ	ꓘ	≣
D	ꙑ	ᛗ	ꙝ	ᚥ		⹀
E	ꙮ	ᛘ	ꙝ	ᚺ	⃫	≣
F	ꙮ	ᛈ	ꙵ	ᚼ	⨂	⊟
G	ꙮ	ᚷ	ꙩ	ᚹ	ᕁ	⧣

Modern	(1)	(2)	(3)	(4)	(5)	(6)
H						
I						
J						
K						
L						
M						
N						
O						
P						
Q						
R						
S						
T						
U						
V						
W						
X						
Y						
Z						

Finally, let me reiterate that when in doubt, create your own symbols; make things that have meaning for you and don't worry about traditional symbols. If you substitute a sigil that has a lot of energy for yourself and your group, it will have more energy and a greater chance of success than a historical one with no personal charge.

Chapter 5
Meanings of the Colors

Some colors seem to have a universal effect or meaning. A well-known example would be "Non-violent Pink," used to calm down violent detainees around the world. Other colors may have a strong racial or cultural element in their effect. For example, in North America and Western Europe, red is automatically viewed as denoting violence and passion, while in China and much of the Orient it is the color of good luck. In our culture, white is seen as representing purity, openness, spirituality and life; in Japan it is the color of death and mourning.

This is best demonstrated by a brief investigation of the "appropriate" color of a culturally significant object, the wedding dress. Most people assume that these garments are white and have always been so. But red, green and blue have, in various locations and periods, been the only appropriate or even acceptable color. Because of these interpretational differences which influence the magical and spiritual color correspondences from culture to culture, it is impossible to say that there is a single "correct" set of meanings for any color. However, it is important for the body artist to choose some set of correspondences in order to begin his/her art.

The Colors and Pigments

Before going on to discuss the meanings of colors, we must agree with what color we mean when we use names such as "brown," "yellow-green" or "purple." I utilize the "Artist's Color Wheel" published by The Color Wheel Company, 1989. Consulting this tool, I will refer to fourteen of the sixteen primary, secondary and intermediate colors, along with seven others. These are: red-violet, red, red-orange, orange, yellow-orange, yellow, yellow-green, green, blue, blue-violet, turquoise (blue-green plus blue), pink (red plus white), brown (orange plus blue), purple (blue plus red), and gray (gray scale value #4), as well as black and white. Additionally, four metal colors have been included.

My personal lexicon begins with interpretations based on Old European meanings for the three most ancient and powerful primary colors: white, black and red. I have supplemented these three primaries with a broad range of other colors, the meanings of which are based on modern Wiccan and Neo-Pagan magical theory. Your choice of meanings, to be effective, must be based on your own belief system and its inherent correspondences. If you are uncertain of the meanings or powers of various colors, consult the references in the bibliography and the following list of the basic color symbolism which I use and teach to my students.

Let us start with white, most commonly-viewed around the world as the color of spirit, nourishment, and "otherness." Traditionally obtained by using kaolin clay, chalk or wood and bone ash, white has come to indicate or induce participation in the sacred rather than profane world or a desire on the part of the wearer to communicate with the world of the spirit(s). It is also used to indicate items whose rightful place is that world of "otherness," as well as possessions by the spirit(s) and Gods. As such it is often used for invocation imagery.

On a different level, white represents the gift of mother's milk, the first source of nutrition. As such it stands for the concept of "provision." It is used in the form of chevrons or stylized clouds in nearly all female fertility rituals—conception, the three trimesters, and birthing—to ensure adequate milk production of the mother-to-be.

Though much maligned in Western culture, black is the color of the night, power, physical strength, death, restriction, fear, and the unknown. Its traditional sources have been either manganese oxide or ground charcoal. When looking at all the different, even contradictory, meanings of black, it is easy to understand why some people are confused or even frightened by it. The one thing that black does not mean is "evil."

In Western culture, at one time death had the meaning of a doorway, passed through in order to reach another place, often of rest and then rebirth. As the color of night, the female time, black is also the color of the powers of woman and of secrecy and magic. It is also the color of physical strength, as seen in the male coming-of-age design where physical growth is recognized and encouraged. Black is also the color of the fear of things that are not understood, but which must be faced. As such, it is one of the colors of the hero, who feels fear but acts boldly.

Red is the color of will, blood, birth, life and energy. Ocher was one of the first three pigments used by our ancestors, and it is the one most widely used today. It is the color of blood and thus the color of life and life energy. It is used to outline the green triangle of fertility in the First Blood Ritual: fertility wrapped in the blood of menarche. Representing life energy, it is used for conception magic, indicating the spark of life that is the beginning of the creation of new life. As the color of birth, it is used in trimester and birthing rituals. Finally, in rites of passage it is used to illustrate descent or parentage via the blood line.

Red is also the color of lust (in its earlier meaning of "overwhelming drive"), of will, and of desire, so it is used to reinforce those feelings. It is also used for symbols that have a different meaning, but which require such drive to be applied. Red is also the primary color of offering and sacrifice. For this reason it is an appropriate color for use in rites of dedication, or ritual hunting rites.

Red-violet combines the spiritual values of the purple family with the forcefulness and power of red. Thus, this intermediate color is appropriate for the spiritual warriors, women and men who seek the path of service to their community or the defense of that community and its members. Since red is the color of offering and sacrifice, red-violet pertains to spiritual sacrifice.

Red-orange is the intermediate most representative of absolute abandon, the allowing of passions to not only flow free but to completely take over. As such it can be useful in the healing process by encouraging catharsis, allowing strong feelings such as rage to overwhelm the subject under controlled circumstances so that healing may take place. However, since this color is so volatile, it must be used most carefully by experienced practitioners.

Orange has often been described as the primary male tone because it is the product of air (yellow) and fire (red), the key male elements. It is an active, demonstrative, high-energy color, used to raise personal energy as well as being the color of courtship. If you really want to draw attention to yourself, wear orange. Orange is also the color of action, physical exertion and sometimes confrontation. It is a great color to use to overcome depression, the February blues, or to generally fire you up. Orange is found directly across the color wheel from turquoise, the primary female color, and is its compliment and reinforcement.

Yellow-orange can be summed up as the color of the intellectual revolutionary. Combining intellect with strong forcefulness and power, it is especially useful as a meditation color and for those preparing to present new and radical ideas, perhaps to an unfriendly audience.

Yellow is the color of the mind, of intellect, memory, attention. Because of its attachment in Western thought to the philosophical element of Air, yellow has come to stand for the powers of the mind. The central point to be kept in mind when dealing with yellow is that it is the color of intellect, curiosity and imagination, rather than practicality.

In representing air as a physical rather than philosophical element, yellow indicates breath and breathing. While it might seem more appropriate to use a light blue to ease difficult breathing conditions, blue is representative of water and may actually cause congestion. Therefore yellow is used in healing works to counteract asthma and other respiratory conditions.

In other cultures, yellow has accrued a wide variety of meanings, ranging from divine communication to the color women use to attract male partners. Before working with yellow it is best for the student to take the time to research the meaning of this color in her/his own belief system or cultural context.

Yellow-green is the shade most appropriate for all types of new growth, new developments, new beginnings, and other processes recently begun. Yellow-green is used in Ostara or Beltane rituals, childhood dedications, and betrothals.

Green is the color of realized fertility, growth, life, riches, and security. Along with brown, green is generally used to indicate or bring about fertility. As such it is used in female coming of age rites, and conception and related rites. It may also be used in supplication for crop or herd fertility. It is an extremely harmonizing color, bringing people to their centers. It has also been used in male mysteries, especially in its aspect of camouflage, serving to hide the hunter from the prey.

Green must be used quite carefully when it comes to healing. As it represents fertility and growth, it can stimulate the growth of fungi, bacteria and viruses, thus seriously raising the risk of severe infection.

Turquoise, which, on the color wheel is the combination of

blue-green and blue, is the product of blue and green, the primary female colors. As such it embodies fluidity, forceful-ness, wild nature, and power of change of water combined with the stability, practicality, fertility and power of resistance of earth. The combination is strong enough to shape planets or bring about life, with the male principles playing but a small part.

Perhaps turquoise can best be understood by comparing it with the "Strength" card in Tarot: a calm acceptance and passive allowance that, in the long run, overcomes all. As such it is often used in female rituals where archetypal imagery is called on, where Goddess energy is invoked, or where the thrust is toward common femaleness.

Blue is the color of emotion, openness, and acceptance. Blue is rarely used in many cultures because it has few natural sources. In North America, blue usually signifies the spirit of the sky, the divine male principle. In Celtic society it indicated a dedication to the divinity, either by someone whose life had been given to the priesthood or someone who was in the process of giving their life to their deity. It is associated with Water, the element of emotion, and also with cooling or with freeing bound fluids. Thus, it is often used in healing magics. An appropriate use of especially the cold, pale shades is to apply them directly to those hot, red, and/or swollen areas of acute infection to counteract the swelling and ease the fever.

Recently, the purple family has taken on the meaning of spiri-tual seeking. Blue-violet, for instance, is the color of the seeker after sacred, divine or spiritual love, agape. For this reason it is not at all unusual to find blue-violet on the Tarot card, "The Hermit."

As a representative of the purely spiritual, we use lavender, a combination of violet and white. This, along with saffron-yel-low, is the traditional color of spiritual peace and under-standing around the world.

The use of a true, deep purple (red plus blue) is much more involved. Purple is the color of royalty and power in the mundane world; it is the color of the emperor. As such it causes the viewer to see the wearer as a powerful leader who is in control of their destiny and, thus, at peace with the world.

Pink is the softer cousin of red. It is used almost exclusively in two types of magickal workings. The first deals with rites of passage such as conception, where pink can be added to the basic design to increase the probability of a daughter rather than a son. It is also sometimes found in childhood dedication rituals and even just before First Blood. In each of these cases the shade is strong yet soft.

Then there are workings which use a brighter, hotter pink. These are rituals of attraction or love. Pale pink is reserved for use in drawing familial or platonic love, strong feelings of attachment but relatively passionless. Deepening the shade increases the level of passion, with the hottest, brightest pinks reserved for lust with a little feeling and caring on the side.

Gray, like white, is a color of other worlds, "otherness" and spirit. Traditionally obtained by using gray clays, partially-oxidized wood ash, or by combining kaolin clay with manganese oxide, gray takes the wearer to the borderland between the everyday world and the world of the spirit. Gray is usually applied to the whole face or even the entire body, thus separating the ego or the entire existence of the wearer from life as we know it. Thus we see gray as one of the most truly powerful and empowering colors with which we can work. As such, we acknowledge that it must be used with much care and consideration.

While green is the color of realized fertility, where the seed of new life has or at least will soon take root, brown is the color of actual but unrealized fertility. Thus it is used for all types of fertility rituals and symbols. This is the color a woman applies to ensure fertility prior to ritualistic conception art. It is the color anyone can apply in order to open themselves to new growth, plowing under the past and offering a new, fertile field for change.

Gold is used to represent the Sun and various solar symbols. It is more allied with the God than with the Goddess, but it has been used for both. Metallic colors are rarely used directly on the body, although a number are safe for most skins. More common is the use of bright metallics in masks and fabric for costumes for specific rites. Brass, bronze and other gold-like colors fall into the general category of gold.

If gold is solar and masculine, silver is viewed as lunar and feminine. As such, it is purely Goddess oriented. This is the reason the vast majority of Pagan and Wiccan jewelry is silver.

Copper is the metallic color of love, expressed in the joining of the Goddess and the God. It is used for both love and fertility workings.

Of course, there are other color interpretations. The Ndembu of Zimbabwe use white to symbolize strength, purity and fertility because it is the color of semen and milk. Red is the color of blood and of life, while black is the color of night, concealment and decay. The Tchikrin, probably the world's most active body-painting peoples today, use color and design daily. Anthropologist Terrence Turner reports that these Amazon Basin people paint themselves for birth and death, for marriage, initiation and all their other spiritual endeavors. For the Tchikrin, white is the color of purity and is rarely used because it isn't part of everyday life. Black is the color of death and, thus, initiation. Boys are covered in black and girls are painted on breasts and thighs at the time that they enter adulthood. Red is the color of life and will for these amazing people.

Every color available to a people takes on one or more attributes. While many of these may be similar from one cultural group to the next because of some particular shared symbolism, there are also examples of a color having completely different, sometimes opposite, meanings. What is essential in the practice of spiritual body art is that you attach specific meanings to each color on your palate. One point that will continue to surface throughout this book is that you should trust your own instincts. Just as the meaning of colors vary from one culture to another, the meanings of colors can vary from individual to individual for any number of reasons, from cultural and ethnic heritage to dreams. If you really want this to work, you have to build a personal understanding of the meanings colors hold for you. Don't be afraid to experiment until you have created a color vocabulary that works for you and for your group.

Chapter 6
Ritual and Makeup

Lying somewhere short of body painting and halfway between painting and masking is a simple tool that a large number of people ignore: ritual makeup. Some feel that the use of makeup is a mundane habit and has no place in ritual. Others claim that since ritual deals with the spiritual, the placing of emphasis of the physical is sacrilegious. As far as each of those positions go, it may be valid. However, since many of you reading this book are interested in the development of a magickal persona, makeup may become a strong adjunct of your rituals.

As anyone who has led a large ritual knows, good ritual is good theater. While it's perfectly acceptable to lack a certain amount of flare or forgo interest-grabbing techniques when you're working alone or even with your regular circle, the same cannot be said when you work with a large or unfamiliar group. No matter how wonderful the ritual, some of the people in attendance are likely to become bored and unfocused after about the first thirty minutes. These people need to feel drawn into the mystery; their attention needs to be caught and held. One way to do this is through the use of dramatic personal makeup. If you're doing a large ritual, wearing no makeup means that the colors and shapes of your face will disappear into a pale blob, due to your distance from the people in the circle. Showing a different face, especially one you have created to set the mood of your ritual, will fascinate them.

There are two types of makeup to be considered: "Operatic makeup" is "normal" makeup applied in the extreme, so as to make the face of the wearer more visible at a distance. The other is "theatrical makeup," which is mostly seen in mystery plays; this is a greater use of makeup, often combined with small props. One ritualistic makeup design as old as Dynastic Egyptian civilization is "the Eye of Horus," probably applied to early kings and queens. A modern example of theatrical makeup is the application of horns and brown grease paint to create a Pan-like appearance. Another is the use of "skin shrink," to give the skin an old and wrinkled look; combine this with a white wig to allow a young woman to enact the role of the Crone.

The use of ritual makeup probably goes far back, at least to early Mediterranean cultures where women led worship and acted as sacred vessels for the Goddess, receiving love and worship in Her place as sexual embodiments of Her. Frescos from Crete and other locations demonstrate the use of makeup by both men and women, though whether this was for ritual or everyday wear is uncertain. Makeup was also used in various shamanistic societies where there was either a requirement for cross-dressing or homosexuality on the part of the shaman or magick worker.

This ritualistic use of makeup is little different from masking or body painting. It can play a major role in the process of self transformation prior to ritual. Similar to body painting, basic designs can be altered to fit various situations or needs. As the makeup is applied the process itself actually triggers the subconscious mind of the wearer. I'm aware of several groups who use such ritual makeup quite heavily, and not only on the High Priestess. Most are affiliated with the Egyptian mystery traditions, though there are numerous exceptions.

Acquiring Your Make-Up Kit

What types of makeup should be used and where can such makeup be purchased? I suggest that you use makeup that has not been tested on laboratory animals. There are alternatives to such testing and there are a number of manufacturers that market animal-friendly makeup. Check what is available to you locally and don't be afraid to ask; the salesperson should know if one particular line of makeup is specifically not tested on laboratory animals and will probably make a point of telling you. Most theatrical makeup is safe in regard to animal testing as governments don't require the same level of safety testing for these as for regular women's cosmetics.

First, find a case to store all of the makeup you're going to purchase, and I don't mean a little makeup bag you can fit in your pocket or purse. Ideally, the case will have a number of levels where you can store all you need to carry and, more importantly, find it when you want it. A very large fishing tackle box with fold-out compartments ensures that everything is immediately visible and none of the smaller items will be crushed.

Go to your neighborhood drug store and forget what the manufacturer had in mind as a use for the products. Some lipsticks make wonderful substitutes for grease paints; some eyeshadows work equally well as highlighters or even partial face colorants. Be creative and, more importantly, give yourself permission to experiment. No one has to see you when you start to play with all these magickal toys (though a second set of hands and eyes can sometimes be a great help).

As for the makeup itself, begin by purchasing as wide a variety of eyebrow and similar pencils as you can find. These will be used to outline various shapes, to draw and color small symbols, and for half a hundred other reasons. You'll easily find blacks, browns and blues, but with some serious looking you'll find other shades as well. Supplement all of these with a dozen or so lip pencils in various shades, and you have the beginning of a kit. You can find these at any drug store, but you can probably do a lot better at a discount makeup outlet. If you are lucky enough to find a bargain outlet, spend time looking through the stock for old Halloween makeup. This usually includes a wide selection of unusual nail colors, grease paints and hair and skin sprays.

Your next stop is a theatrical costume and makeup shop. The prices at these shops are higher, but so is the quality of the makeup they handle. What you'll be looking for here are grease paints (in as many shades as possible, as many of them don't mix well), water-based hair color (liquid or spray), and, perhaps, a wig or other items that strike you. Find a white makeup pencil and, since they have at least a hundred uses, don't stop at one—buy at least half a dozen.

My Kit

A brief look at my makeup kit might offer some ideas. In it there are a dozen makeup sponges, various brushes, cotton balls and cotton swabs. Then there are two or three bottles of cold cream and cleansing cream, a bottle of mineral oil, a strong herbal facial scrub, and a bottle of astringent cleanser.

Next there are at least half a dozen bottles of hair tip colorants in a wide range of colors, along with an equal number of mascaras. These are supplemented by a variety of lipsticks in "normal" shades as well as some unusual colors such as blue, green, yellow, and orange, accompanied by matching nail colors. I also carry a number of tubes and spray cans of hair and skin colors and color sticks, which are like children's crayons, usually a clear base containing colored metallic flecks.

Then there are grease paints, lip pencils and crayons, and eyebrow pencils. Finally, there are about fifty shades of eye shadow. On top of all of this are my tempera paints, brushes, and other items I use for more extensive ritual body art, as well as my own personal colors, made of hand-ground pigments in a neutral base. I also carry a pair of small goat horns which I use for male mysteries rituals and mystery plays. These were purchased for a dollar from a local butcher shop. To these I recently added a pair of Halloween latex werewolf ears which help create a very magickal "Pan-like" appearance.

When I am doing extensive ritual decoration, at a festival for instance, I carry along several stainless steel bowls for rinsing brushes, some soft rags to touch up runs or mistakes, a can of art-fix to spray over the work once it's complete to make it last a little longer and, finally, a can of spray insect repellant.

Make Your Own

One friend, involved with a Sumerian-oriented group, goes so far as to make eye makeup in the traditional manner, from Lapis Lazuli ground to the consistency of talcum powder, applied like normal eye shadow. If you'd like to make your own paints, the simplest way is to purchase pre-ground pigments at a local art supply store, or begin with dry tempera colors available at a children's or school supply store. Remember that some art store pigments, such as lead oxide and chrome, can be quite unhealthy. If you're not sure, ask the person behind the counter or stick to the dry tempera colors. Mix these with a medium of your choice, such as a lanolin creme. You won't need too many different pigments to begin with as you'll probably be dealing with basic primary colors.

If you or your group are interested in experimenting in creating various types of makeup, one good source for all natural makeup is Jeanne Rose's *Herbal Beauty Secrets*. This volume has a wide variety of recipes that are safe, natural, and can be altered to meet your and ritual needs.

Hair

There's one other area that should be considered by both men and women: hair. Traditionally, people have used hair color, length and arrangement to indicate social status, vocation, etc. Now is the time to bring your hair into line with all the other work into which you have put so much effort. If you are involving yourself in a Norse type of ritual, braid your hair and, if you're married, put the braids up. Women have, for eons, indicated their status by the binding or not binding of their hair. You can use this to indicate either your status or the aspect of the Goddess you wish to represent or contact: bound hair for the Maiden versus free hair for the Mother, or rebound hair for the Crone. For example, in a ritual dedicated to Diana the Huntress, women may present with their hair braided tightly in a single braid. This braid is then tucked under or doubled over so that their hair is completely out of the way. In a handfasting, part of the ritual may be the letting down of the bride's hair, indicating her changed status.

Due to the current male fashion of short hair, most men have few styles to choose from but, should their hair be long enough there are several options. A male counterpart to the woman in a Norse ritual would wear the majority of his hair free but with a single braid on each side at the front, framing his face. A number of cultures, including nearly all Native American societies, feature male hair kept in the opposite manner as that of women: free as a child, bound as an adult, and free again in later years. As to color, that is up to you. There are several good quality temporary hair colorants on the market. With these it is possible for Mother Earth to appear with flowing green hair, a few flowers held by two or three small braids, crowned by a chaplet of flowers. If, by just reading this description and visualizing the scene, you felt something, think how such a real image would affect people attending a ritual where a proper setting and mood have been created!

Chapter 7
Masks and Masking

A mask is similar to temporary art because it can be removed when no longer needed for ritual celebration. A mask is also similar to permanent body art because it maintains a constant design, though often for far longer than cicatrization or tattooing because a mask can be passed from one generation to another.

Though masking is a later development than body art, masks have long been associated with the sacred. An example of the mask as a ritual tool can be found in the story of the Medusa in Greek mythology. Classical Greeks used masks in theater, a practice which dated from much earlier. We also know that theater began as a purely religious ritual. These two facts, taken with one or two points in the story of Perseus, such as his nailing of the Medusa's head to the shield of Athena and, later, to the prow of a ship, suggest that in fact the "head" of the Medusa was a sacred mask. Such a mask would have been a cult object of an earlier, Goddess-worshipping people, passed down from priestess to priestess, each of whom, when she put on the mask, assumed the persona of the Goddess in an unchanging way.

Collaboration of this type of practice is provided by a great number of indigenous peoples. From the Zuni we have the Kachina masks, full-face masks that, when donned, put the wearer in touch with the spirit of the mask and the power or archetype that it represents. The Hopi provide us with the example of the Mudheads, adobe spirit masks that act in the same manner as the Kachina. In the Great Lakes region, various Algonquin peoples still use a wooden mask carved from a living tree, in order to retain the spirit of life. They add corn husks or other materials in the place of hair, providing a full head covering.

Becoming the Mask

Masks allow the wearer to "step aside" so that the energy of the mask and the force that the mask represents may flow through them. The wearer becomes a prop, holding up the face of the divine. He becomes the mouth that is used to speak the divine words, a divine puppet, moved by the hands of the Gods, a channel between the people and their Gods.

Anyone who has ever put on a mask has felt, at least in a mild way, this alteration of consciousness. Actors who have worn masks for various productions will tell you that the putting on of the mask accomplishes the change from actor to character in just a few seconds, which can often take an hour or more when only makeup is worn. Masking also serves to put distance between the person wearing the mask and the audience. It allows the wearer to be equitable and dispassionate, removes the fear of criticism or retribution, and allows them to open fully and without fear to the powers of the mask and the forces which move it and give it voice.

Neo-Pagans are starting to re-discover the mask and some of its uses though, at present, the practice of masking is still in its infancy. Masks are still primarily used as disguise when individuals prefer to remain anonymous while taking part in public rituals. These masks can be made into powerful magickal tools and should be created rather than bought. Although it is perfectly correct to start with a commercial mask, add to it until it is a reflection of your magickal persona. For those of you who have a totem animal, your mask should reflect that totem. If you have a particular matron or patron, apply the symbols and colors of that deity to show that you identify with Her or Him. You may also want to include a coven symbol or sigil, done with the consent of the group. A variation of this theme is the construction of coven masks that serve to identify you as part of that particular group. In this case the design should reflect the soul of the group in some way.

In Neo-Pagan mystery plays, masks enhance effective instructional theater, which is the purpose of such productions. However, I have observed that even in these performances the masks rarely attain their potential. This is not the fault of either the mask or the person wearing it. Instead, it is due to the tentative nature that pervades our community. In order to reach its maximum potential, to take on life, a mask must be allowed to come alive—the spirit of the mask must be allowed to take over the person on whom it rides.

Masking must be learned anew as two interrelated acts: first, the donning of a mask as an act of invocation or evocation, a summoning of divine forces into the primary position in the body, mind and spirit of the wearer. Second, the donning of a mask constitutes an act of rejection of all that Eliade refers to as the "profane," mundane reality. The wearer must have enough confidence in self and faith in the Gods to completely relax the ego and become a tool of the Gods, just as surely as is the mask. Profane rules and codes of behavior must be entirely set aside, for the mask has its own set of rules, often quite unlike our feeble human structures and restrictions.

Another appropriate use for masks is in coven or inner circle sabbat and esbat rituals. In such a setting, working with trained initiates, a mask can exert its full force. Here, amidst the love and the trust of the group, the wearer can yield up the ego and become one with the spirit. In this secure setting, all present, masked and unmasked, can receive the full benefit of the energy that works through the mask. The divinatory and prophetic spirit may be brought to its fullest; the great teaching spirits may be heard and truly understood; the wildness of life can be allowed to run loose. Such a setting is appropriate for other reasons as well: all the members of the group have experience dealing with forces greater than themselves and all know how to ground the energy that is raised. Should such a group be asked to perform a ritual at a festival or gathering, they can do so masked, bringing to the ritual much more of this gift of the Gods, being secure in one another and their shared experience.

The Basic Masks

Though one mask can have several uses, a savings in funds and work, it is actually better to have a separate mask for each energy/force/deity. This is because the mask will, over time, absorb the energy it serves. Using a mask for more than one focus will dilute the different energies with which it is used.

Begin by creating three Goddess crown masks: Maiden, Mother and Crone. Gather a variety of wreaths in vine, straw or other material, as well as plants and flowers, real and artificial. If you choose to use natural material, all the better, but if you make the crown in advance or if you have to pack it away to travel to your ritual site, you may have a problem: when you go to put it on, your flowers will be wilted, your grain broken and you will be busy chasing flies away from decomposing fruit!

The Maiden mask could be so simple as to not even be a mask, but rather a crown of flowers with a white or pastel veil attached to provide partial covering for the face. The mask for the Mother can be similar to that of the Maiden, but with the crown made of grain and fruit rather than flowers, and the veil being in a primary color. Finally, the Crone mask or crown should be of braided vine or willow and decorated with autumn leaves or herbs. It should possess several layered veils, most of them black, although the inner, hidden layer could be white, silver, or gold.

The use of veiled masks with painted faces is quite powerful. The face should be painted first, lowering the ego and setting the stage for the invocation or evocation that will be triggered by the placing of the mask.

Essential male masks begin with the traditional foliate mask of Britain. This mask is based on a commercial full-face mask or a home-made plaster or papier-mache mask, painted in shades of green and covered with real or fabric leaves of various types, acorns and other nuts, berries, even flowers if you like. If you create the mask in such a way that these objects can be attached and removed easily, the mask can be altered to reflect the seasons.

Another basic male mask is the golden-faced Sun or Young Lord mask, sometimes referred to as a "mask of Apollo." This may be a full-face mask, or it may leave the lower face uncovered. This mask also does well made in several pieces: the upper face, the mandible, and additional pieces such as a flared outer border (representative of the Sun), a crown or wig of grain, and other appropriate items that could be added and removed so that it could work for a variety of rituals.

Finally, a revel mask personifying the Bacchus/Dionysus aspect of the God would be a good investment of effort. A jolly mask, bright-nosed and round-faced, with a crown of grapes, is appropriate as an alternative mask for the harvest festivals of Lammas and Mabon, to serve as the Lord of Misrule at Yule, and to encourage the gaiety and celebration of Beltane.

Making Your Masks

Begin by sketching the mask you wish to create or by finding

a picture from which to work. It doesn't have to be accurate; it simply has to show you the general look. Some practical considerations to keep in mind while you are designing and creating your mask include your vision—how well will you be able to see when wearing the mask? How about comfort—could you wear this mask comfortably for the two or even three hours that large rituals sometimes take? Then there's effectiveness—you've created this mask for a reason, how well does it meet this goal? And affordability—some items are very expensive, but with a little substitution and imagination there's no reason why you can't create a mask that will look like your ideal.

For the creation of these masks, you'll require a human model, some petroleum jelly, a couple of drinking straws, and the mask material. The foundation mask can be made with plaster bandage (available from most hobby stores and some drug stores), low-temperature-hardening modelling clay, or even old fashioned papier-mache (strips of newspaper soaked in a mixture of flour and water).

The next step is to prepare the model. If you're using plaster bandage, this is done by applying petroleum jelly to the model's face and the leading edges of the hairline. Have the model insert the straws into his/her nose so that he/she will be able to breathe while the rest of the face is covered with the modelling material. Then, begin building your mask. Soak several rolls of plaster bandages, cut into manageable lengths of about six inches to a foot, in warm water. When soft, apply the bandages to the face. Press each strip firmly onto the face or previous strip so that the shape is true and joints are well bonded. The first layer is just a foundation, so don't try to accomplish any detailing with it. Just make it comfortable for your model. If you're using papier-mache, the steps are exactly the same, but you'll want to be sure to build a foundation thick enough to be sturdy. After this stage of the mask has dried, remove it from the model and allow it to season for about a week.

If you're using a modelling clay material, the process is somewhat different. First, instead of using petroleum jelly, apply a fine layer of talc, chalk, flour or cornstarch to the face of your model. Straws for breathing aren't necessary because you can cut out breathing holes as soon as the clay is applied. Next, roll out a sheet of your material approximately one quarter of an inch thick. Apply this to your model, taking time to mold it to the face. Press the material down firmly to outline the eyes, mouth, and other facial features. Add most of your basic detailing while the material is still damp and pliable. When you are done, carefully remove the mask and follow the printed directions for hardening the material.

The second stage, adding the persona to the mask, is accomplished by adding any number of details. For instance, for the foliate mask, you'll want to make a trip to your hobby store for paints but, while you're there, pick up several sprigs of fabric leaves to apply using epoxy or simple white glue. For other masks, use your imagination: foil, flowers, sequins, glitter, vine wreaths, and nearly any other material you may need are all readily available. Experiment!

Another popular material for masks is leather, although it takes a little practice to achieve really outstanding results. A particularly stunning use of leather is in the creation of the foliate mask, especially when time and patience are exercised. I have seen a number of leather ritual masks that are both beautiful and durable.

For a leather mask you'll need a good grade of fairly thin oak-tanned tooling leather and a "male" mold of a face—a life-sized casting of a face to which you can attach the wet leather with tacks. Wet the leather, lay it over the mold and stretch it into place—this will take some practice. Once you've created the basic face in the center of your piece of leather, let your imagination free to fold, bend, twist, and stretch the edges of the piece into whatever shapes you wish. Then allow the leather to dry for three to five days before spraying with a waterproofing agent. Remove the mask from the mold. It may now be colored with spray finishes or an air brush.

Consecrating Your Masks

Once you've created your mask, cleanse and consecrate it just as you would any other magickal tool. Be careful when cleansing it with fire because many materials such as feathers, are quite flammable. Be wary of candles and bonfires as well; it would be a shame to lose so much work and energy, but worse to have it catch fire while you were wearing it! Be cautious cleansing it with water, too, because some dyes on commercial items are water soluble and may run. An easy way to prevent both of these problems is to treat the mask with flameproofing and waterproofing agents.

Here is a mask consecrating ritual that you may wish to use to cleanse and consecrate your mask and to prepare it to be used in a ritual context. This ritual is appropriate for use in consecrating a personal ritual mask or mask of disguise. Following this complete ritual are the sections, as indicated, which should be substituted in the cleansing and consecration of a sacred or sabbat mask.

CASTING THE CIRCLE

O thou circle, thrice traced, thrice blessed, shield us ever against wickedness and evil. Protect ye the power which shall be raised within your confines this night. In this, by the sacred names of our Lady and our Lord, I do consecrate thee and bless thee and this place which you contain. So mote it be.

ASPURGENCES

With the sweet breath of life I do cleanse, consecrate, and bless this circle that it may be a fitting place for our worship of our Lady and our Lord. So mote it be.

With the hot flame of desire I do cleanse, consecrate, and

bless this circle that it may be a fitting place for our worship of our Lady and our Lord. So mote it be.

With the flowing waters of love I do cleanse, consecrate, and bless this circle that it may be a fitting place for our worship of our Lady and our Lord. So mote it be.

With the fertile earth of wisdom I do cleanse, consecrate, and bless this circle that it may be a fitting place for our worship of our Lady and our Lord. So mote it be.

CALLING OF THE GUARDIANS

I summon, stir, and call thee up, o ye mighty ones of the east, to guard this circle and witness this rite and bless that working I work this night.

I summon, stir, and call thee up, o ye mighty ones of the south, to guard this circle and witness this rite and bless that working I work this night.

I summon, stir, and call thee up, o ye mighty ones of the west, to guard this circle and witness this rite and bless that working I work this night.

I summon, stir, and call thee up, o ye mighty ones of the north, to guard this circle and witness this rite and bless that working I work this night.

GODDESS INVOCATION

I will sing of Thee, Mother of all, eldest of things. You feed all creatures that are in the world, that go lightly upon the lands, that are in the paths of the seas, that fly across the skies. Through You are we blessed; to You it belongs to take these things away. Happy are we whom You delight to bless; full are our spirits, our souls and our lives. Thus it is that we pray You visit us with Your presence, wisdom and blessings.

GOD INVOCATION

I will sing of thee Father, Lover and Beloved of Her. Your fire of life lives in all creatures that are in the world, that go lightly upon the lands, that are in the paths of the seas, that fly across the skies. Through You are we

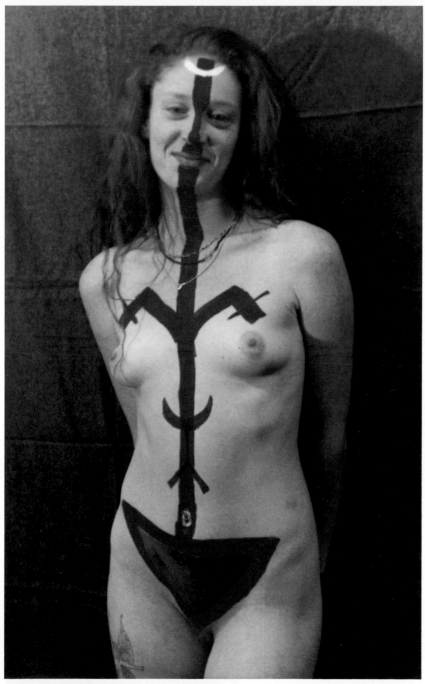

1: Female Coming of Age.

The designs portrayed in this section are described in Chapter 12.

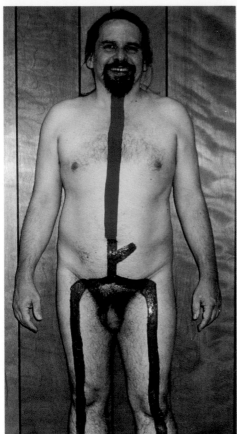

2: Male Fertility.

3: Strength.

4: Female Fertility.

5: Pregnancy, First Trimester.

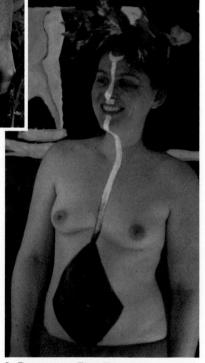

6: Pregnancy, First Trimester.

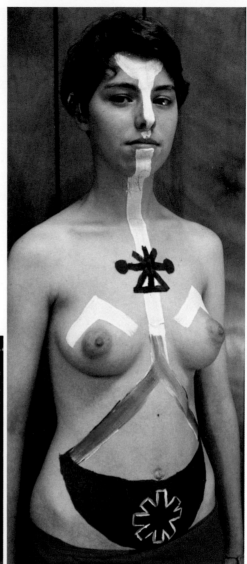

7: Pregnancy, Second Trimester.

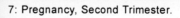

8: Pregnancy, Second Trimester.

9: Pregnancy, Third Trimester.

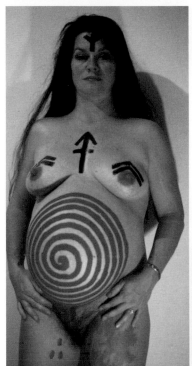

10: Direct Birthing.

11: Indirect Birthing.

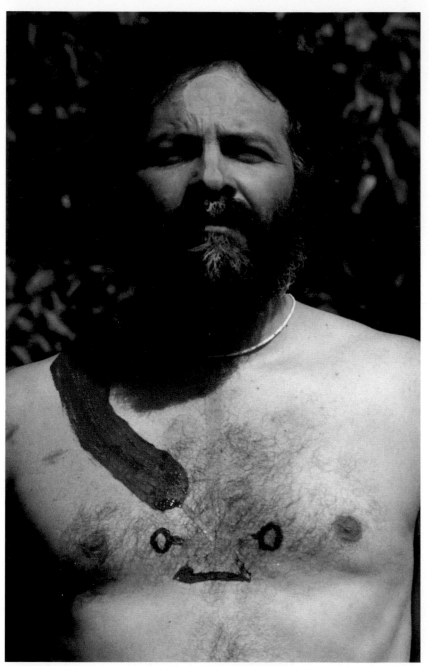

12: Adoption.

13: Mourning, Miscarriage.

14: Mourning, Miscarriage.

15: Mourning, Abortion.

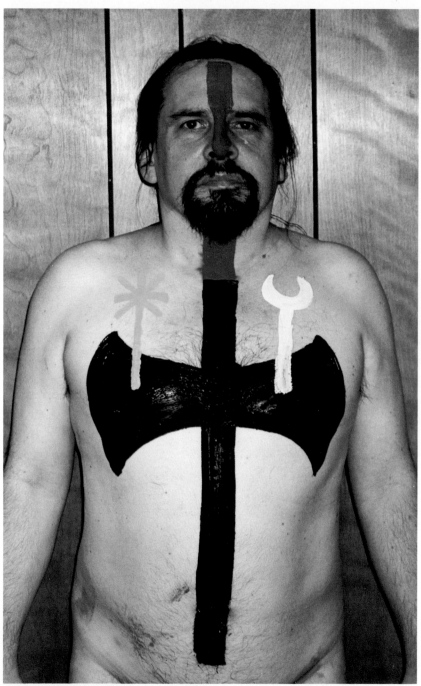

16: Death.

17: Handfasting.

18: Handfasting.

19: The Goddess as the Prime Female
Force.

20: The Goddess as the Lady of the
Moon.

21: Male Hieros Gamos as
the Green God.

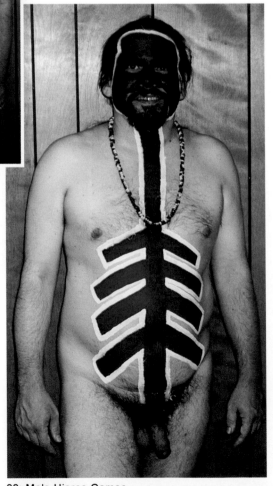

22: Male Hieros Gamos.

23: Female Hieros Gamos.

24: Male Hieros Gamos.

blessed; to You belongs knowledge of the Dance of Life. Happy are we whom You delight to honor; fertile the fields you seed. Happy are we whom You delight to bless. Thus it is that we pray You visit us with Your presence, wisdom and blessings.

MASK CLEANSING

With this sweet incense I do cleanse and bless this mask of my magickal self—may it be imbued with thy intelligence and imagination. So mote it be.

With this hot flame I do cleanse and bless this mask of my magickal self—may it be imbued with thy will and passion. So mote it be.

With these flowing waters I do cleanse and bless this mask of my magickal self—may it be imbued with thy love and healing. So mote it be.

With this fertile earth I do cleanse and bless this mask of my magickal self—may it be imbued with thy strength and wisdom. So mote it be.

MASK CONSECRATION

Mask of spirit, face of my magickal self, I conjure thee to protect me from all who would reveal me as a Hidden Child of the Goddess. I conjure thee to take unto yourself that self that lies hidden from the world of men but shines forth in the realms of the Mighty. Aid me in the service of the Gods and my sisters and brothers of the Craft. Open my eyes that I may see; open my ears that I may hear; guard my mouth that I may never reveal the secrets which have been given to me. By fire and air, water and earth I conjure thee that within thee shall remain no adverse thought or enmity. Hear my will, attend to me as I will. So mote it be.

Paint your magickal name or sigil on the inside of the mask over the third eye, chanting: "Blessed be thou face of my true self."

FAREWELL TO THE GODDESS

Mother Goddess who is the Earth itself, provider for Her children, we have called and You have come forth and witnessed our love, respect and worship for you. For this and for all other gifts, both known and unknown, we thank you and bid you hail and farewell.

FAREWELL TO THE GOD

Father, lover and beloved of Her, teacher of the dance of life, we have called and You have come forth and witnessed our love, respect and worship for you. For this and for all other gifts, both known and unknown, we thank you and bid you hail and farewell.

FAREWELLS TO THE GUARDIANS

Great guardian of the North, Power of the forces of earth, you have been with us this night, protector and guardian and witness in our worship of the Gods. Depart you now for fairer places, hail and farewell.

Great guardian of the West, Power of the forces of water, you have been with us this night, protector and guardian and witness in our worship of the Gods. Depart you now for fairer places, hail and farewell.

Great guardian of the South, Power of the forces of fire, you have been with us this night, protector and guardian and witness in our worship of the Gods. Depart you now for fairer places, hail and farewell.

Great guardian of the East, Power of the forces of air, you have been with us this night, protector and guardian and witness in our worship of the Gods. Depart you now for fairer places, hail and farewell.

BANISHING CIRCLE

This circle is now ended. We leave with beauty and love in our hearts.

Chapter 8
Ritual Apparel and Props

I f body coloring and masks are not only ritual objects, but also aids in the alteration of consciousness and the bringing forth of the magical persona, then so too must be the robes or costumes, jewelry and any other objects worn during ritual. Whether it's an Enochian "Robe of Glory" and its cover, a simple tabard, some specially-created gown, a special set of what would otherwise be dress clothes, or even a negligee or loin cloth, any of these can serve as ritual attire. These items prepare the wearer to enter into an alternate reality, an alternate level of experience in the land of the sacred. Think back to how you felt when you put on your Sunday School suit—it made you feel just a little different, didn't it? That was probably your first inkling of the process of ritual transformation.

And, lest the more Pagan of us feel left out, the same holds true for going into ritual skyclad. For those who are taught that we should enter the sacred circle clothed only in the glory of the Goddess, it is that same glory that gives free range to the imagination.

The shedding of your everyday persona and dressing in a sacred garment, mask, makeup or jewelry is taking up a different level of life. And, when experienced in this way, the donning of a robe or any of these is an act of evocation/invocation as well as a first step into the world of the sacred.

Robe Wardrobe

I'm often approached by students wanting suggestions concerning appropriate robes, but I find it hard to give specific answers. The robe should be appropriate for the wearer and the group, if any, with which she/he works. For some, a caftan is appropriate, but for others, such as those who practice the Fivefold Kiss of reverence, the robe must open or in some other way allow access to the front of the body.

I currently possess three robes, all black. The first is nothing more than a piece of black cotton cloth, directly off of the bolt, three yards long and hemmed at either end. I have cut a slash neck and hemmed that as well. I wear this tabard-like, with a cord around my waist holding either both parts to me, or just the front, allowing the rear to flow behind like a cape.

The second was purchased from a costume shop where, for years, it was rented out each June to graduating students. It is a heavy silk academic robe (the likes of which are available in a number of colors). It has a hook and eye at the neck but no other closures so, with just a cord around it, it's quite acceptable no matter what group I work with.

Finally, my last robe was purchased specifically as a ritual robe from a seamstress who creates such garments. Any major Pagan gathering will usually include at least one or two such businesses, exhibiting their wares, which often come in quite a wide variety.

It is good to create robes for various seasons or types of rites. For mid-winter a white robe, perhaps with silver trim, is quite nice, especially if you take the time to add an under layer of dark brown, indicative of the fertile earth resting under the snow and ice. In the spring women often appear wearing robes of willow or light green, yellow, purple and other flower colors. Of equal power are bright yellow robes for men. Later, dark brown apparel especially for women, again representative of the earth, are often seen. Come summer, if robes are seen at all they are often as bright as nature around them. Reds, greens, blues and yellows abound. And when autumn rolls around, the colors take on a fullness and richness equal to that of the fields. Harvestide celebrations are often full of oranges, golds, dark reds, and dark greens, the colors of the fields, the crops and the trees. Finally, toward the end of the old Celtic year, Samhain, black becomes almost universal, although we still see the old farm colors of dark brown, dark green and dark grey.

Nearly everyone I know prefers natural fibre materials for their robes: cotton, silk, linen, or lined wool. A few people (who are either extremely talented or who know someone who is) go to further lengths, ensuring that their materials are colored with natural dyes and often hand spun and hand woven as well. Such robes might be the ideal but I prefer to use ritual dress that suits me and suits the ritual, giving such concerns preference over even the type of fibre. The most important concern is that all the material and items worn fit your magickal persona that constantly lives in that "other place" and "other time"; that part of your psyche that you become when you enter into in this altered state.

I use the term "robes" in the broadest sense. Robes need not be the highly formal creations that one often sees. In one instance, one of my students attended a Samhain ritual in the guise of the Maiden, dressed only in seven veils, each being a square yard of some gauzy material. These were in layers, the first veil brown and covering the front of her body. To this, in an overlapping manner, were pinned each of the other six veils, all light green. The final result was astonishing.

Other Items

How far you go is up to you. When I have been asked to do the makeup for the cast of a large outdoor mystery play, I've applied body paintings, used masks when they were available, and used my makeup kit to create the mood and the magick of a ritual.

In one case I helped a young woman personify the element Water. She was already wearing a wonderfully shimmering blue gown and cloak. She had applied blue eye shadow, which I didn't feel was appropriate, so I removed it and replaced it with green. I then painted her nails a dark blue, colored her hair a mix of blue and green plus some opalescent sparkle, outlined her hair with blue and gold liner, and colored her lips a deep turquoise. It seemed to work. Sometime between doing her eyes and outlining her hair, the young lady faded away and was replaced by a sea nymph that all who attended the ritual saw by the light of the bonfire. More importantly, that is what everyone there experienced; the young lady's essence included the words, thoughts and feelings of a water elemental come to life.

"Chaplet" is the formal term for a wreath or similar piece of headgear. These are common enough articles at Pagan celebrations but, with a little planning they can become much more. One can easily create a chaplet that will correspond to a particular Goddess aspect, season, or mystery play role. By taking a small commercial wreath, available from a craft supply store, and adding real or silk flowers, herbs, fruit and vegetables, or other items such as decorative snowflakes, you can create a chaplet that will enhance any ritual. If the idea of using imitation items surprises you or makes you uncomfortable, by all means use the real thing. However, when travelling long distances, crossing borders, or encountering other difficulties, the imitation items will stand you in good stead.

A veil can be added to a chaplet or used on its own. Veils can be used to portray different aspects of the Goddess, hide the identity of the wearer, or even to demonstrate something of the nature of the mystery that lies behind Goddess worship. The type and color of material will depend on the use to which the veil is to be put. If you work with a group on a regular basis, it would be well to invest in a number of swatches of cloth, each perhaps only a yard or two, of several suitable types of material which can be hemmed and used as needed. Two black and two white veils, one of each color sheer and one opaque, make a good beginning. The black can be used to represent the mystical aspect of ritual, the Crone, and the female aspect generally. The white can represent the glory of the Goddess, the Maiden, and, when worn under a black veil, enlightenment. Add to your stock as time goes by, purchasing to meet needs as they arise.

The same for chaplets, as long as you're willing to use artificial decorations. Starting with two or three wreaths, purchased or hand made in willow or grape, collect silk flowers of various colors, silk leaves of green and autumn colors, plastic fruit and any other items that strike your fancy, along with a spool of florist's wire. You can create chaplets to meet your needs, then take them apart and store the decorative items until they are next needed.

And, while we're on the topic of ritual props, don't forget a cornucopia or other seasonal items. These, too, can be found at craft supply stores and discount stores as well as garage sales and flea markets, and, with just a little imagination, can readily be altered to suit your needs.

Chapter 9
Ritual Jewelry

In addition to robes, masks, and all the other objects already mentioned, there are a series of other items which help to create, empower and carry on magick. I refer to that most common of all magickal adornments: jewelry.

A necklace is a strand of beads or similar items hung about the neck, which generally tend to be of a uniform or graduated size and continue for the length of the necklace. A pendant, on the other hand, is one large item hung individually on a chain or thong; although a pendant is sometimes hung from a necklace. In Goddess-centered worship, the necklace is a symbol of initiation or rebirth, although the exact meaning is up to you or your group. A pendant, on the other hand, can be used for nearly anything, ranging from a magickal talisman to a pendulum weight. It can be any item which helps the wearer identify with the ritual and forces called upon.

Rings are used widely for magickal or transformative work. They are chosen by metal, design, or stone or to bring the special properties of that metal or stone to bear on the work at hand. Rings are also important to set a psychological mood, to act as a focal object in trance work, as a sort of battery to catch and store energy until the wearer needs it.

The metals from which personal ornaments are made have particular properties. Gold is solar, more allied with the God than with the Goddess, but it has been used for both. Silver, on the other hand, is viewed as lunar, purely Goddess-oriented. Copper is the metal of love and is used for both love and fertility charms. Iron, when it is worn, is used to contain energies, harness will, and to protect the wearer from attack by the Sidhe, the dwellers in Fairey. Other metals such brass, platinum and tin may also be worn, but this is usually done only after long study into their magickal properties.

Rings are also made of wood, horn, antler, and various cut stones. Oak rings are generally the most magically powerful, although a willow ring is said to instill great insight during divination. Ash rings strengthen courage, while a ring made from elder brings peace to the soul. A ring of apple wood brings love. Rings of hoof, horn or antler are usually only worn by those involved in Hunting Mysteries and represent the sacred duality of hunter and hunted, killer and killed.

The Stones

As for the stones to be set in your jewelry, here is a short listing of the esoteric properties of a variety of stones.

Agate. There are a wide variety of agates and each should be treated separately. Banded Agates have long been held to attract physical and emotional strength to the wearer. Blue Lace Agate calms, soothes and attracts happiness and emotional peace. Moss Agates balance personal energies, with the green working on physical energies and the white focused on emotional energies. Botswana Agates, with their soft pinks, grays and purples, are healers of the emotions and the spirit. The opposite effect, energizing the body, mind and spirit, is accomplished by natural Crazy Lace Agates.

Alexandrite is sacred to the divine hermaphrodite. This color-changing stone bridges the gap between male and female. For this reason it is nearly mandatory on occasions when a person of a different sex performs in a gender-specific role.

Amber is one of the sacred stones of ancient Egypt. Because it is vegetable rather than mineral in origin, it is said to possess unusual magickal properties, especially the accumulation and storage of energy. For this reason, amber makes perfect ritual jewelry. It has a history of being associated with long life.

Amethyst is said to provide additional spiritual strength and to help the wearer sleep more deeply and dream more clearly. It also brings about constancy in love. For centuries amethyst was thought to prevent drunkenness. It was also claimed that amethyst could neutralize poisons, which is patently false.

Angelite, a recently discovered, soft blue stone, has been found to be cooling and calming and has strong healing effect on muscular cramps.

Anthracite, ordinary hard coal, represents the continued usefulness of the elders of the community and the importance of family and community traditions.

Aquamarine is the epitome of female power, combining the cool blue and green feminine colors in a hard stone with incredible brilliance. This is also a healing stone, especially for the removal of fevers, regeneration of tissue and eradication of inflammation.

Aventurine, usually a pale or jade green but sometimes a greenish turquoise, is a strongly-defined female power stone, also effective for new beginnings.

Bloodstone is often found in the first aid kits of metaphysical healers as it slows or stops the flow of blood. Psychically, it is used to stop the flow of personal energy in order to counter

psychic vampirism.

Carnelian, the opposite of bloodstone, speeds up blood flow, helps raise blood pressure and may raise adrenalin levels. It also serves as a charm against various types of enchantments.

Citrine is the bright yellow relative of the amethyst. Citrine serves as an aid to study and learning and may be used to help ease migraine headaches, the inability to concentrate, and writer's block.

Corals are animal in origin. They have been used for their magickal properties for thousands of years. Red Coral is said to promote long life and curb impotence. When ground and applied directly, it heals skin ulcers. Black Coral is said to be one of the supreme power stones, especially when working with forces of Water. White Coral is often given as a token of affection. Be cautious using coral because many are endangered and much of the Red and Black Coral on the market is imitation.

Diamond promotes purity and constancy of affection and reinforces one's strength of purpose. Unfortunately, diamonds also absorb energy from their surroundings and store not only the energy but the emotions which generated it. For that reason they have to be cleansed in salt about once every solar month.

Emerald is a stone sacred to the ancient Mayas and the Incas. The most expensive stone in the world, Emerald helps to calm strong emotions, aids in plant and animal fertility, and is said to bring riches. Emeralds have also been attributed with improving the memory and intelligence. For some reason, emeralds have also been claimed to protect the wearer from rape.

Garnet was sacred to the Egyptians and to the Babylonians,

Greeks and Romans. Garnets aid in bringing on menstruation as well as conception, depending on the intent of the wearer.

Fluorite is a truly amazing stone, multi-faceted with an octa-hedronal shape and having colors varying from clear to pale blue, yellow and purple. Some stones came with two or even three colors. Metaphysically, fluorite embodies strength, control and unflappability on a variety of levels, depending on the color of the stone.

Hematite is often found worn by professional psychics. The most powerful of all the grounding stones, hematite keeps the wearer firmly in the "here and now" despite all the energies around him/her. It also reinforces the will of the wearer.

Jade is considered the concentrated essence of love. Jade also aids in plant and human fertility. It is supposed to deflect bad luck from the wearer, often breaking in the process. It embodies wisdom, modesty, courage, justice and charity.

Jasper is powerful and mystical. Each stone must be chosen by the wearer, not picked by another and given as a gift. Every color has a use (refer to Chapter 5). Fancy Jasper, which combines soft pinks, pale mauves, muted greens and a variety of other colors, is used to create harmony, peace and understanding.

Jet is a power stone sacred to the Goddess in Her Crone aspect. It calms hysteria and helps bring an end to hallucinations.

Lapis Lazuli was sacred to nearly every major early culture. Lapis is mentioned in the Inanna texts as well as in early Egyptian writings. The unusual combination of blue, white and gold marks it as a weather stone as well as a dreaming stone. It is said to bring an end to depression and melancholy

and to bring good luck.

Lodestone is not beautiful but it is a good magickal material with which to work because it attracts energy better than amber, though it doesn't hold it as well. For this reason, it is one of the most effective stones in combatting psychic attack.

Malachite is a two-toned green stone that aids in reestablishing the fertility cycle, better for plant fertility than for animal (including human).

Moonstone is sacred to the Goddess, especially in Her Mother aspect. As such, it provides protection during pregnancy and delivery. It embodies the powers of the moon, affecting menstrual cycles and body clocks. It is said to improve psychic abilities.

Obsidian or Volcanic Glass comes in black and dark green. It serves as a sharpening focus for sight and an aid for incisive action. Snowflake Obsidian is black with white inclusions. It works to reinforce the character of the individual caught up in difficult or trying circumstances.

Opals are probably the most misunderstood of all stones. Popular opinion holds that Opals bring bad luck, but nothing could be further from the truth. These wonderful stones unlock incredible power related directly to their type; White, Black, Jelly and Fire. Additionally, opals offer immense aid to those who would work with magick in that they speed up the wheel of karma for the wearer. This assists the true student to learn more rapidly from experiences. Anyone who puts an opal on will be in for turbulent times, both seemingly positive and negative. Karma gained over years of actions will come very rapidly but once the backlog has run its course, life becomes much simpler.

As personal power stones, each type of opal has a particular

strength and should be used for different work. Black Opals relate to power within the context of nature, as well as magnifying intuition. The much more common White Opal (often referred to incorrectly as a Fire Opal) aids in cleansing the aura and helping the wearer to understand their own karma as well as that of others. The rare Jelly Opal, the clear type which shows its colors more softly, serves as a potent storage cell for healing energy and aids the wearer in all types of elemental magick. Mexican Fire Opals, which combine a high-energy orange with a strong and peaceful purple, help blend force of will with peace. For this reason they are particularly appropriate for negotiators, arbitrators and councilors.

Pearls, like Coral, are an organic item. These products of clams, mussels and oysters are feminine in aspect. They tend to bring the wearer into closer harmony with the tides of the world and into greater consciousness with living things. Long thought to bring bad fortune, pearls merely focus the state of the world in the consciousness of the wearer, often bringing pain and suffering.

Peridot is a pale green stone that aids plant fertility and attracts the Maiden aspect of the Goddess. It is useful to bring about new growth in plants, personal projects, and a wide variety of other fields limited only by the imagination of the user.

Petrified Wood. Like amber, the product of long dead living matter, petrified wood symbolizes eternity, in that the individual may die but life will continue. Petrified wood is often given at coming of age rituals.

Quartz. As a white or clear crystal, quartz is one of the most overrated of all stones due to the marketing of New Age entrepreneurs. Quartz is like a Swiss Army knife—somewhat helpful for nearly any task, but not particularly powerful nor well suited for any one, except, perhaps, as a focus for meditation. Rose Quartz, the soft pink stone of love, is used to attract long-term love, a lover as well as friends. Smoky Quartz combines "sight" with power and practicality, so it is suited to those who engage in the various psychic arts.

Rhodonite is a hard stone which combines the pink of strong attraction with the grey and black of otherness and reality. For this reason it is the perfect gift for someone who attracts the wrong kind of partners. It can be used for magickal workings where the goal is for the subject to attract the kind of partner they really need, rather than the inappropriate types they are usually drawn to.

Ruby is a lovely, rich and very expensive stone, sacred to the Babylonians. It aids menstruation, seals loves, and brings on enhanced animal fertility.

Sapphire. Brilliant blue, it assists in mental clarity and acuity and aids the wearer in becoming more discriminating in the choice of acquaintances and activities.

Selenite, especially selenite roses, found in soft pinks and peaches, offer their aid to those seeking new beginnings where healing lost loves is essential.

Sodalite is often mistaken for lapis lazuli. It is a dark blue stone suited as a storage battery for emotions and emotional energy.

Sugilite is the most peaceful yet powerful, tranquil yet commanding stone, especially the opaque variety. The deep purples combined with the usually soft, smooth surfaces instill peace, understanding, and courage.

Tiger's Eye is generally noted for aiding in the development of psychic sight, as well as granting limited psychic protection. The only natural type of Tiger's Eye is gold, which gives the bearer the power to see reality more clearly and precisely. The other types of this stone are all colored using a combination of heat and chemicals. While such stones may strike the reader as unnatural, each has a specific magickal strength. Red Tiger's Eye aids the holder to see through the will of others, thus rendering their magick more visible and more easily overcome. Blue Tiger's Eye is used in situations where someone wishes to see clearly but feels that their emotions or the emotions of others cloud their view of reality. Finally, Green Tiger's Eye gives the wearer the power to see truth and strength in persons or in objects, even when it is not obvious to others. Likewise, this stone can also be used to detect lies, falsehoods and weakness.

Topaz, stone of knowledge and wisdom, is usually considered a masculine stone unless of the Royal Topaz variety, in which the shade changes from a bright yellow to a peach or pink.

Turquoise is one of the most sacred and powerful stones of the Americas. This piece of sky fallen to earth, with its wonderful feminine colors, brings on calm, promotes peace between female and male and makes a wonderful personal power stone.

Unakite makes a perfect focus for creating new life, combining as it does both a reddish brown and a green.

Objects that are viewed as ritual or power objects by their owners often are worn only in a ritual setting. If they are worn at any other time, it is usually in an attempt to draw on the energy stored in them or to draw on their ability as tools of consciousness alteration.

I do want to suggest one or two guidelines about wearing rings. First, more than three rings on any one finger is considered tacky. Second, wearing so much jewelry that you can't lift your arms is tacky too. Third, when you go out to buy ritual jewelry, get the best no matter what the material. If you need a ring of iron for some reason, make sure it's iron (bond the inner surface so that your finger won't get covered with rust). If you need silver, get sterling or pure silver. German or nickel silver isn't appropriate because there isn't a bit of silver in it. It usually consists of nickel and steel though, sometimes, other metals may be added as well. And lastly, there is nothing wrong with insuring your jewelry.

used in addition to the scent medium, the energy created increases synergistically. So this way of decoration should never be used on someone who does not have adequate experience in psychic self-protection.

By adding scents to paints, it is possible to subtly shade the meanings of the colors and symbols, making them more accurate, appropriate and powerful. Here's a list of some of the simple scents that I use, along with a short description of their effects and some color correspondences.

Allspice is a heating scent that will add fire to the work of projecting will. Allspice can be used in place of red and for the symbols of Accomplishment, Sending Energy, Fight and Gain, To Strive and Overcome, and for Perseverance and Strength.

Almond has a variety of uses, the most common of which is as a base for other scents. Alone it is a calming scent used to bring peace. It can be used to symbolize Childhood.

Amber is a strong solar scent with a male orientation, often used in oils for the summer sabbats as well as for a power base.

Ambergris should be used sparingly as it is a strong attractant and, when mixed with musk and civet, a strong aphrodisiac. This scent is most appropriate replacing bright pink and the signs Attraction, Create Desire, all Fertility symbols, and Sexual Union.

Apple Blossom, a traditional beauty scent, is often used as one of the oils of the First Blood ritual. It adds compassion and tenderness as well as luminescent beauty. It readily substitutes for the colors white and pink and signifies, the Unborn Child, Children, Daughter, Dream, Girl, Happiness, Joy, Love, Peace, Pregnancy, Purification and Wholeness. Apples were considered by the Celts to be sacred to the Goddess, thus it plays an important role in invocation of nearly all of the Celtic goddesses.

Balsam is the first of the evergreens, all of which, with the exception of cedar, represent the element of Air and are used for purification and in young male ritual works.

Basil is one of the most common household herbs. It is often forgotten that it, like many other scents of this type, has magickal uses. Like bay, basil is used for purification of a space as well as promoting harmony and a sense of family.

Bay is a strong purifier used in rituals that call for the removal of ego. The color black and the symbols for Purification and Change are those most replaced or reinforced by this scent.

Benzoin is a sweet astringent. Another strong purifier, it should be used sparingly, mostly for male rituals. The color is bright blue and the symbols most often associated are Male Friends, Partnership, Purification and Removal of Suffering.

Birch is probably the most common of all aids to communication and is used any time understanding is the goal.

Blessed Thistle is used as a purifier in spiritual and psychic healings, to consecrate sacred spaces and objects, and as an olfactory invitation to deity.

Blueberry has traditionally been used at Lithia by the Blueberry Maiden. It is appropriate for all celebrations.

Boneset is used for its magickal properties as well as scent. The name says it all: boneset is applied directly over breaks to help speed the mending process.

Camphor, when used carefully, is a stimulant and energizer which combines the elements of Air and Fire. It is also used whenever a healing ritual focuses on breathing problems or respiratory infections.

Carnation is a strong healing scent that also raises the level of awareness. For this reason it is especially appropriate for use in rites of passage. Carnations are most often found in red and white, and these are the colors that this scent most adequately replaces. Carnation symbolizes Childbirth, Comfort, Healing, Initiation, Intuition, Marriage, Passage, Release of the Soul, and Spirit.

Cedar is the scent of both Purification and Dedication, especially of the body, to the works of the Gods. It may serve as an attractant as well, but only to those who have achieved a certain level of subtlety and spiritual awareness. Cedar doesn't replace a color. Rather, it replaces a whole segment of the spectrum from yellow (communications) to blue (loving), and green (healing and fertility). Because cedar is an evergreen, one would think that its basic alignment is masculine but, in fact, it's feminine. Cedar symbolizes Family, Friends, both female and male, Honor, Perseverance, Practicality, Protection, Stability, Strength, and Unity.

Chamomile is a strong calming agent often used in healing rituals.

Chili is a powerful scent which may irritate the lungs. As an oil it can cause blistering. However, used in small quantities it is the strongest of the Solar/Fire scents, a strong energizer which can also serve as a powerful repellent.

Cinnamon, like allspice, is a heating oil, one which tends to draw forth the true will of the person being painted. While cinnamon may be used in the place of red, a more appropriate

‡ ※ △ ◊ ✳ □ N ※ ✳ ▽ ◈ ß △ ⅄ Γ Ρ ⊖ ⊳ ⊞ ⚹ △

correspondence is orange. Cinnamon symbolism includes Enthusiasm, Fire, Invocation of the God aspect, Maleness, Man, Overcoming, Self, Strength, Strength to Summon, and Victory.

Civet is the most base of the sexual attractants and should rarely be used alone because it is a provoker of uncontrolled lust. However, under controlled circumstances it may be used alone in small quantities to bring out the feline, stalking nature that makes a skilled hunter. Civet crosses the color wheel from red to green, creating a little brown along the way. Its signs are Sexual Desire, Femaleness, Animal and Human Fertility, Maleness, and Sexual Union.

Clove is one of the strongest of the Solar scents. It can be used to invigorate the listless, supply energy for physical, mental or spiritual work. A word of warning: clove oil, if concentrated enough, can burn sensitive or even normal skin, especially in hot weather or under direct sunlight.

Clover is a young scent, often used to stimulate the Maiden or Young Lord aspect during evocation of the divine from within. It is also used in rituals and rites devoted to the subject of growth.

Coffee as a scent is just as much of a stimulant as is the drink. It, like chocolate, was sacred to various south and central American deities.

Copal is an ancient incense whose scent purifies and conse-crates both objects and spaces.

Cubeb is a little known and rarely used key to the strongest aphrodisiacal scents. Its spicy, musky smell is truly a turn-on.

 (102)

Cucumber is one of the primary Water elemental scents. Light, cool and refreshing, it is used for all Water alignment rituals as well as for healing inflammations or to stimulate fluid production within the body.

Deer's Tongue serves as a purifier as well as, when used as an incense, a visual representation of prayer. Another interesting aspect of this scent is that it reinforces the speaking of truth in rituals or ceremonies and in day-to-day life.

Dragon's Blood is probably the foremost of all the "Power" scents. Many people imagine the scent to be very strong, possibly offensive. In fact, like anything possessing true power and strength, the scent of Dragon's Blood is soft, even delicate.

Eucalyptus is as healer of various breathing disorders. Secondarily, eucalyptus is used to raise endurance levels, especially physical endurance.

Frankincense, a deeply spiritual scent appropriate for nearly any occasion because of its protective qualities. Amber and saffron are the shades that this scent replaces and Dream, Invocation of both Goddess and God, and Prayer (Supplication) are the symbols associated with frankincense.

Gardenia is a calming and purifying scent used to prevent or overcome panic or hysteria.

Ginger, except for chili, is the strongest of the Solar scents. It will counter listlessness and may supply energy for physical, mental or spiritual work. Ginger oil can burn the skin, especially in hot weather or under direct sunlight.

Hawthorne, along with Witch Hazel, is the scent of the Earth

Witch and brings groundedness to the wearer as well as the ability to stimulate plant fertility. It is often used in crop growing rituals.

Heather is unusual in that, while it is an attractant when worn by a woman, it is a strengthener of will when worn by a man. For women it also holds calming and reinforcing properties. For men it strengthens resolve and aids the defensive warrior.

Heliotrope is one of the major Solar scents, so it is used for all Solar rituals, in male coming of age rituals, and a wide variety of other celebrations. It is also effective against depression and seasonal disorder.

Honey is the perfect food, the treat of the gods. Honey scent is used in rituals in which one dedicates one's life to the gods, or in other acts of sacred profession, as invocation. For this reason, as well as for its strength as an attractant, it is also appropriate as a scent for the Hieros Gamos (Great Rite).

Honeysuckle is a sweet, innocent scent that is both feminine and solar. It is a pleasant reliever of tensions and fears. Honeysuckle may be used as a grounding scent, bringing a heightened consciousness to the physical level, and as a mild attractant. It readily replaces gold, deep green and white as well as the symbols for Change, Growth, Home, Protection, Provision, Removal of Suffering, Stability, Wholeness and Wisdom.

Hyacinth is a sweet pacifier, widely used as an identifier in gay male Wiccan covens. It is also particularly appropriate for use at Ostara.

Hyssop, a psychic cleansing scent, is for any type of purification or deep meditation. It is also appropriate for mixing with the base color when other scents are mixed with pigments for

power symbols. Hyssop does not replace any particular color, but it is particularly appropriate for the symbols Dream, Initiation, Invocations of both Goddess and God, Spirit and Wisdom.

Juniper, that smell behind gin, has several uses, the most important of which is the appeasement of karma and the attraction of beneficial forces. In other words, "good luck."

Lady's Mantle as an applied scent has a calming and protective effect. It has been said that Lady's Mantle can make the wearer invisible in times of danger.

Lavender is strong and calming with protective overtones. Some people react unfavorably to lavender because of memories associated with this scent, such as grieving or pain, because the scent was used by a mother or grandmother. It symbolizes Air, Healing, Offering, Order, Past, Protection, and Wholeness.

Lemon will clear away dreams and instill a zest for life, an excitement for living. Lemon is yellow, and its principal symbolism is Air. Others include Enthusiasm, Decrease of Flow, Travel and Wish. I prefer lemon juice to the oil because it's sharper and cleaner, without the sweetness.

Lilac is one of the strongest of all emotionally calming scents. Its sweet scent can be used in nearly all situations where gentle love and acceptance are the goals.

Lime is a vitalizer and a cleanser. Its sweet sharpness heightens the senses, lightens the step and adds new acuity to ones life view. It is effective against depression, rouses the sleeper and adds its own particular zest to life.

Lotus has long been used to alter consciousness. It is also used

to increase psychic awareness and so is appropriate for deep meditation and similar work. Lotus may, in a pinch, be used to replace blue, green, yellow or white, but it really isn't a color scent at all. It symbolizes Increase of Flow, Intuition, Release of the Soul, Spirit, and Water.

Magnolia is a dark, heady seducer which will slowly overcome all resistance. As such it is one of the primary sexual power scents.

Mandrake is the most powerful of all the Earth scents and must be used carefully. It is capable of incredible grounding, aids in all types of physical fertility, and is the prime scents of the hunter and warrior.

Mastic is the gift of Selene, Lady of the Moon. It is appropriate at all times when the full power of the Moon is being sought.

Melon is a light scent used to combat both fevers and "hot bloodedness." It, along with cucumber, is among the strongest representatives of Water.

Mimosa is similar to magnolia though it is slightly less potent and adds a little more of the element Air to its seductive cloud.

Mint is a calming agent as well as a purifier. However, when using mint oils on the body one needs to exercise caution as some members of the mint family such as Wintergreen can cause burning and irritation.

Mistletoe is, of course, the courting herb and its scent is used for just such activities; to indicate interest, etc.

Mugwort is one of the most powerful aromatic agents for the

stimulation of divinatory talents. As such, this scent readily replaces gray and silver and may be used for violet as well. Mugwort doesn't carry a specific meaning, but it may be used in meditation before deciding what type of scents, sigils and/or colors to use in your work.

Musk, light and dark, are sensual scents, drawing from and calling to the more primitive aspects. Musk oil is appropriate for raising power. Light Musk is especially useful in the First Blood ritual, mixed with the green pigment used to create the fertility triangle. Musks cover a range of colors: hot deep reds, black, rich dark browns, and deep pinks and roses. Musk symbolizes Attraction, Earth, Femaleness, all the Fertilities, Learning, Offering, Sexual Union, Wife and Woman.

Myrrh is a deeply spiritual scent that is useful for altering the levels of consciousness. Associated with the Moon and the Goddess, it is also mildly protective of the psyche and the body. Black, white and silver are the colors for this scent, and Childbirth, Dream, Femaleness, Flow (both increase and decrease), Invocation of the Goddess and Woman are its symbols.

Narcissus is a mystical scent that will speed a seeker on his/-her journey. This oil, when used carefully, is applied to the paint to be used on the face, assisting the coloring that will erase the ego and allow the subject to experience "otherness." Narcissus is best used to represent black and symbolizes Change, Death, Disruption, Future, Invocation, Learning, and Wisdom.

Nutmeg is another hot, spicy, sweet solar scent that strengthens will. Nutmeg also carries with it several thousands of years of tradition as an enhancer of male sexual performance and curer of impotence.

Oak Moss, one of the most earthy of all the scents, is appropriate for hunters, the sacred lovers, and those seeking harmony with the Earth and its cycles. Obviously, this scent stands in for brown and the deeper shades of green, as well as Defense, Earth, Family, Plant Fertility, Growth, Harvest, Home, Order, Present, Stability and Strength.

Olive. No work with any Greek or Roman deity should be done without using olive oil either singularly or as a base for nearly any type of magickal scent. However, olive does have one drawback: a rather strong and even offensive scent that the skin absorbs easily and rapidly.

Orange Blossom is a sweet, attractive yet purifying scent that is appropriate on any occasion when softness is called for. The color is pink and the symbols are nearly the same as for apple blossom: Children, Daughter, Girl, Happiness, Joy, Love, and Wholeness.

Orchid is an incredibly potent attractant of divine attention and stimulus of spiritual power. It tends to calm the wearer but should be used sparingly by anyone with their feet not firmly planted in the earth.

Orris has been used for centuries for magickal formulas. It is one of the more potent power scents though it is understated and easily camouflaged.

Patchouli is the most popular Earth scent. Along with an attractant, it is part of nearly all fertility work. It is a strong grounding substance and should be used with a soft compliment as a cushion. Patchouli is one of the basic oils that should be included in the kit of anyone working with scent magic. Like Oak Moss, the color replacements are browns and dark greens, and it shares many of the same symbols such as Earth, Plant Fertility, Growth, Harvest, Present, Stability, Strength, Maleness, Man and Husband.

Peony is a sweet, gentle and potent scent that adds the power of gentle persuasion to any and all work.

Pine. The cleansing scent of pine and its evergreen cousins, balsam and spruce, clear the mind, free the soul, and let the spirit soar on the winds blowing through the forests. Pine is a good balance to patchouli or Oak Moss for Earth magics, and replaces nearly all shades of green. Pine symbolizes Air, Boy, Enthusiasm, Healing, Honor, Intuition, Learning, Purification, Removal of Suffering, and Volunteer.

Rose is a wonderful attractant and so much more than that. The mystical symbolism of the rose is often forgotten these days, but the rose is one of the most potent magical symbols and scents in the entire western world. This scent is appropriate for nearly any type of magickal work. Anyone seriously interested in scents would do well to study the various types of roses and their symbolisms over the centuries. Obviously, then, rose can substitute for several colors, excepting only green, blue and brown. Rose can readily replace nearly any symbol.

Rosemary is yet another cleanser and purifier commonly found in most homes.

Sandalwood, symbolizing purity, a gift to the Gods, has been used for thousands of years as a religious offering. The use of sandalwood calls on the deepest spiritual forces, without and within, and elevates the soul while providing strong protection. White, purple, violet, gold and deep blue are the colors this scent most appropriately replaces and its symbols include Intuition, Movement, Present, and Retreat.

Spruce. You can learn most of what you need to know about spruce by reading the comments on the other evergreens.

Sweetgrass has long been used as a purifier by Native Ameri-

cans. The smoke of burning sweetgrass is seen as the physical form of prayer.

Thuja, or *Cedar Leaf Oil,* is a purifier of incredible power and should be used sparingly. It can be used for the most powerful magickal works, including the banishing of spirits and the negation of magickal attack.

True Unicorn Root does not have much of a smell other than a rather generic plant scent. It is one of the few scents which works directly to cure impotence or improve male sexual performance.

Vanilla is an attractant, but in a homey way. This is a good scent to use with pinks and browns when working to attract a male mate.

Vetivert is a green, bright, strong, living, growing green: the power of fertility brought into vibrant action. It is the next step after the earth scents such as patchouli or Oak Moss.

Violet is a softening smell, used to bring about physical, emotional or spiritual peace.

Wintergreen is the strongest of all the evergreen scents. While it can represent Air, it is most strongly used as an analgesic or in various scent blends for winter.

Witch Hazel, either as an oil or as the normal pharmaceutical preparation, is a purifier and a calming agent.

Ylang-ylang, one of the sweetest of the sensual oils and sexual attractants, rests on the knife's edge. Use it alone, and it can attract passion; mix with sandalwood and Oak Moss or patchouli and it brings the sensuality of the earth itself. Mix it with cinnamon and civet, and it's an aphrodisiac. This scent most closely parallels a deep pink and can adequately replace nearly all of the female symbols as well as symbols of Attraction and Desirability.

A word of warning: as the essences in these oils are much more reactive than either the bases or pigments of most body paints, caution must be exercised during their application. Heating oils such as cinnamon and clove can burn sensitive skin, while others can provoke strong allergic reactions. Care must be taken in their use. Ask the person being painted if she/he reacts to any oils. If uncertain, use the same testing technique as is used for paint: apply a minute amount of the oil in question to the inside of the arm and wait for at least 10 minutes before deciding whether to proceed. If a person reacts negatively to one oil, there are others that you will be able to substitute.

Aromatic Recipes

More power may be generated by combining simple scents synergistically to create a more potent formula. Here are some of my own recipes:

Birthing Oil

This scent, in addition to strengthening the birthing mother and easing the process, will ease the pain associated with labor.

1 part rose	1 part rosemary
1 part sage	1 part sandalwood
1 part violet	

Coming of Age Oil

Generally used to anoint young men in their Coming of Age Ritual, but may be used in any personal empowerment working.

| 1 part cinnamon | 1 part lemon |
| 1 part musk | 3 parts oak moss |

Conception Oil

Assists in conceiving children but may also be used at the beginnings of new projects.

1 part dragons blood	1 part jasmine
1 part mandrake	1 part mastic
1 part patchouli	1 part sandalwood
1 part rose	1 part vanilla
1 part vetivert	

Croning Oil

Generally used in a menopause ritual but also appropriate for a parallel male ritual.

| 2 parts cypress | 2 parts jasmine |
| 2 parts myrrh | 1 part sage |

First Blood Oil

Used for female First Blood or Coming of Age rites.

| 5 parts apple blossom | 1 part cinnamon |
| 1 part civet | 1 part patchouli |

Handfasting Oil

Applied to the couple during the joining ceremony to sanctify the union.

| 3 parts amber | 1 part civet |
| 1 part musk | 3 parts patchouli |

Handparting Oil

To cleanse and purify the wound between the former partners.

3 parts amber   1 part citron
1 part oak moss

Initiation Oil

This oil was specially created for use in traditional Wiccan initiations.

9 parts ambergris   40 parts chypre
3 parts civet   40 parts jasmine
3 parts mandrake   21 parts lotus
21 parts mastic   3 parts mimosa
7 parts mistletoe   7 parts musk
9 parts patchouli   21 parts rose
40 parts sandalwood   9 parts thuja
7 parts vetivert

Passing Oil

To anoint the body of the one who has passed beyond this life.

1 part cedar   1 part cinnamon
1 part Low John   1 part myrrh

Here are recipes for the five different oils which are used for elemental identification and attunements:

Air Oil

5 parts lavender   1 part thuja
3 parts sandalwood

Fire Oil

3 parts cinnamon   1 part civet
1 part clove   2 parts rosemary

Water Oil

1 part ambergris   1 part jasmine
2 parts lotus   3 parts melon

Earth Oil

1 part mandrake   1 part musk
1 part oak moss   1 part patchouli

Spirit Oil

1 part frankincense   1 part myrrh
1 part sandalwood

Here is a collection of oil recipes for the Sabbats:

Samhain Oil

1 part mugwort   1 part myrrh
1 part mimosa   1 part narcissus
1 part vervain

Yule Oil

1 part allspice   1 part holly
1 part orange   1 part pine
1 part wintergreen

Imbolc/Candlemas Oil

1 part lemon   1 part menthol
1 part musk   1 part patchouli
1 part wintergreen

Eostre/Ostara Oil

5 parts apple   3 parts lemon
5 parts lily   1 part lime

5 parts mimosa	5 parts oak moss
2 parts orange	5 parts patchouli

Beltane Oil

5 parts rose	3 parts lotus
3 parts oak moss	2 parts light musk
2 parts patchouli	2 parts cedar
2 parts sandalwood	2 parts civet
92 parts ambergris	1 part light honey

Lithia Oil

1 part apple	1 part heather
1 part mistletoe	1 part oak moss

Lammas Oil

1 part amber	1 part vetivert
2 parts heliotrope	6 parts clover

Mabon/Harvestide Oil

1 part clover	3 parts vetivert
1 part patchouli	1 part frankincense

Finally, a few other recipes which may prove to be useful for your day-to-day work:

Deep Meditation Oil

5 parts sandalwood	5 parts hyssop
3 parts narcissus	2 parts benzoin
1 part lotus	1 part oak moss
1 part patchouli	1 part ambergris
1 part rose	

Fertility Oil

2 parts patchouli   2 parts oak moss
2 parts rose   1 part musk
1 part lotus   1 part cinnamon

Hieros Gamos Oil

Used in preparation for conception as well as during the Sacred Marriage.

3 parts light musk   2 parts oak moss
2 parts ambergris   2 parts dark honey
2 parts light honey   1 part dark musk
1 part civet   1 part ylang-ylang

Peace Oil

1 part rose   1 part oak moss
1 part lotus

Protection Oil

1 part jasmine   1 part lemon
1 part myrrh   1 part patchouli
1 part sandalwood

Purification Oil

2 parts hyssop   1 part rose
2 parts sage

Sacred Warrior Oil

3 parts oak moss   3 parts bay
3 parts cedar   1 part patchouli
1 part cinnamon   1 part benzoin
1 part civet   1 part allspice

Here are a few suppliers of high quality oils at good prices:

The Mother Tree, P.O. Box 610663, San Jose, CA, 95161-0663

Ravenwood Oils, P.O. Box 4258, Traverse City, MI, 49685, 1-800-777-5021

Sacred Spirit Oils supplied by White Light Pentacles/Sacred Spirit Products, P.O. Box 8163, Salem, MA, 01971-8163, 1-800-627-8379

Here are a few brands of very good oils which can be found at your local health food or herb shop: Aura, Casia, Auroshikha, Lotus Light and Sumeru Garden.

Chapter 11
The Setting for Ritual Body Art

Are there times of the month or of the year when body decoration is more effective than others? Are there ways to imbue your work with more energy and, in turn, multiply your probability of success? For thousands of years our ancestors gathered to celebrate the circle of life at certain times. These times, like the symbols, are foci for vast amounts of energy. Here is some information about these times, how they may best be used, and some of the names by which they have been known.

The Festivals

The first of the traditional power times, and one of the oldest of all holidays, is Samhain. Samhain is celebrated from sunset, October 31, to the following sunrise or sunset. Other names for this occasion are Calan Gaeaf, Halloween, and All Hallows Eve. Samhain is a feast to the dead (as is practiced in Mexico), but it is also a celebration of the beginning of life. Magicks focusing on farewells to the dead and working through attendant grief are common, as is magic designed to aid in the conception of new life.

The next celebration is Yule, held from the sundown before the longest night of the year to the following sunrise or sunset.

Yule is also referred to as An Fheill-Shlinnein, Alban Arthan, or Giula (or Geola). Yule is a celebration of birth and new beginnings as well as of friendship, caring and giving. The magicks attached to it focus on enduring good luck, easy births, and courtship.

Imbolc is the sweetest and homiest of celebrations, focusing as it does on children, the family and healing. Celebrated from sunset, February 1, to the following sunrise or sunset, Imbolc is also known as Candlemas, Oimelc, or Brigid, and is equivalent with the ancient Roman celebration of Lupercalia.

Next around the year comes Eostre, the celebration of the Vernal Equinox, otherwise known as Lady Day, Co-Thad-Thrath, Alban Eilir, and Ostara. This sabbat relates to puberty and to new beginnings. If female coming-of-age rites are celebrated as a group rather than on an individual basis, this is a good time for it. This is also the time to do work for the fertility of crops in the coming season.

Next comes Beltane, the other most ancient of holidays, celebrated from sunset on April 30 until sunrise of May 1, or through that day as well. This is the great celebration of life and new life, of sensuality and sexuality. It's also the time to do work for animal fertility for the coming year. This is a traditional time for marriage and handfasting, entering into partnership and purifying old agreements. Other names for this joyous celebration include Bel-tuinn, Walpurgisnicht, May Eve, Cyntefyn, Roodmass and Cetshamain.

Lithia is the first summer festival, held over the night of the Summer Solstice. Otherwise known as Grian-Stad, Alban Hefin, and Midsummer, this is one of the nights of Faerie, when the Good Neighbors come out to celebrate. It's a time to generate and celebrate "otherness," a time of great joy and wild magicks. Other work focuses on attainment of maturity (often through the acceptance of the child within) and with physical strength or agility.

Sunset of the last night of July brings Lammas, the great fire festival, a time to remove debris from your life, and strengthen or reinforce your will. Lammas is also known as Lughnasadh or August Eve.

The traditional harvest festival is Mabon, named after the Welsh "Child of Promise." Celebrated at the time of the Autumnal Equinox, Mabon may also be known as Harvestide, Alban Elfed, or Harvest Home. This is a time for giving thanks and storing up energy for the times to come. Croning celebrations are often held at this time as well.

The Moons

The time to gain strengths or attributes has traditionally been related to the time of the waxing Moon, the period between the new and the full Moon. The waning Moon (the time between the full and the dark Moon) is used to lessen or remove unwanted influences. The night of the full Moon has been seen throughout history, and probably prehistory as well, as the time of greatest feminine power and fertility. The night of the new or dark of the Moon is best for secrets, divination and the alteration of consciousness.

The best time of night for working with lunar forces is when the Moon is at its highest point in the sky. On nights when the Moon rises either very early or very late, or when it is occluded by clouds, start your work so that midnight will occur as close to the middle of your ritual as possible.

The Rites

There are traditional times for ritual work and ways to go about celebrations. Ritual is a tool for accessing and triggering the subconscious. This, in turn, frees the energy and the creative force in us so that we may focus that energy on our goal. You must take time in advance to decide what you want to do,

120

how you want to do it, and when and where it is to be done. The better your preparations, the more successful your ritual will be in reaching the life energy that is stored in each of us, and the more likely you will achieve your goals.

In preparing for ritual, there are things to consider, such as what types of actions best focus your energies on your goals and what type of sacred space you want to create. Once you begin to discuss these aspects, you can flesh out the ritual outlined below with specific words and actions.

The first questions to ask are simple and straightforward: Why are you planning this ritual? Is it designed to be a celebration of life or one of its passages, or is it to work magick? What will be your goals? Are you sure a ritual to aid in the accomplishment of those goals is appropriate? Is this the appropriate time to engage in such a ritual?

The next questions concern who will be attending the ritual: Should it be open to the community or only to some certain portion thereof? Would it be more effective to limit attendance to members of your own group? Perhaps attendance should be limited strictly to the subjects and the ritual leaders?

Certain rituals such as the celebration of First Blood are usually open to all adult female members of the community. In the case of handfastings, the guest list is the responsibility of the couple, rather than of those officiating. The best way to reach a decision on this matter is to discuss it with those with whom you will be working.

Then ask the following questions: What type or types of magic will you work with in the ritual? Will you use color, symbol and scent? Will you use other magicks, such as visualization? Do you have reason to use magickal tools, such as poppets, candles, cords, talismans? How will any of these be used? What will each be expected to accomplish? In what order will you use the tools chosen?

What sacred forces most personify the forces with which you

wish to work? Will you call on the Gods to aid your work or will you use your own energies? Need you call on the Guardians of the Quarters for their energies? If you call for divine assistance, will you need both female and male aspects or would only one be appropriate for your working? Whether you call on one or both aspects of deity, what aspects, if any, will you invoke? In other words, what God names will you use in this ritual? And, finally, will you invoke or evoke these forces—will you call these forces from outside of yourself, from within, or both?

There are literally thousands of different rituals to choose from. (Examples can be found in the books listed in the sources section.) Here is an outline for building any ritual you desire, followed by one sample ritual.

This is a typical order of events within a ritual. You will decide whether to use all of these points or to exclude some and add others. You are also free to rearrange them to serve your will.

1. Construction of sacred space

2. Cleansing and consecration of space

3. Calling of guardians, elements, etc.

4. Calling forth of deities and sacred forces

5. Magical working

6. Sacred meal

7. Farewells to the deities, etc.

8. Farewells to the guardians, etc.

9. Removal of the confines of the sacred space

Once this is decided, you can go on to flesh out your ritual. Decisions here include, but are not limited to, whether you will use prayer, songs, chanting, or dance to call for divine intercession and raise the energy needed for the work.

What scent or combination of scents of incense will you use?

If you use more than one, will you combine them or will you use certain ones at specific times in your ritual?

What colors will be highlighted and how? If you work robed, would you change the colors of your robes for this ritual or would you prefer to use the colors of the candles on your altar to achieve this same result?

Another way to fine tune the focus of a ritual is through decoration with natural objects: flowers, leaves, grain, fruit and vegetables. While the use of such items may be purely decorative, another option would be their inclusion in the sacred meal, in which colors, flavors and scents may play a role.

How will people be expected to dress for the ritual? Will that be left up to them or will it be decided in advance? The alternatives here range widely, from allowing each person to wear whatever they find most comfortable to encouraging the wearing of street clothes, on to robes, and finally, requiring the entire group to practice skyclad.

For those of you uncomfortable with this level of organization or who prefer to work more spontaneously, the questions are much simpler. Will the event be completely spontaneous or will it require some pre-planning? Remember, if you need supplies of any sort, there will have to be some planning in advance. Who will be in charge of working with the energy?

While all of this probably sounds incredibly complicated, it is only as much so as you allow it to become. It's all up to you. Do highly intricate, involved rituals better allow you to feel the life force within you, the energy that you will use to weave the web of magic? Or do you prefer extremely simple rituals? Do you prefer to work alone or with others? In what settings do you feel closest to life and nature? These are the real questions—everything else is foam on the wave.

A Ritual

The following ritual is taken from an eclectic Pagan organization, The Temple of the Elder Faiths, of Toronto.

SUMMONS

This is the call for the group to come together and begin to focus their energies on what will follow.

> The moon is right and our hearts call out, beckoning us forth from drudgery and shackles. Let us break free and join together in that secret place where earth and moon and Goddess wait to set us free. Come, it is time to feast and sing, play and love, to open our souls to the Lady and worship Her in the old ways, as She willed long ago.

SWEEPING CHANT

The area is ritually cleaned of all the cares of the day. All of the worries that people may have carried into the ritual in their subconscious are swept away.

> Stick of broom, stick of doom, sweep your way around this room.
>
> Sweep out pain, sweep out ill, sweep a place that She may fill.
>
> Touch not hope, touch not love, from below or from above.
>
> Leave here peace, leave here mirth, in this circle on the earth.
>
> Sweep out hate, sweep out pain, until we call you up again.

CASTING THE CIRCLE

Once the area has been cleansed, the time has come to create a sacred space by tracing a circle, clockwise, or "deosil," around the group and its chosen working area. This may be

done using the hand, a wand made of a branch, or any other item as long as it focuses your concentration into a narrow beam.

> Life is all a circle that around and within us turns. The circle is the pathway, leading through death and life. On this pathway we must travel; through this circle we must pass.

ASPURGENCES

This is the second cleansing, done after the sacred space has been established. It uses the four principal elements: air, fire, water and earth. To do this, carry the element around the circumference of the circle, and, in the case of water and earth, sprinkling some on the ground as you go.

Carrying incense:

> With the sweet breath of life I do cleanse, consecrate and bless this circle that it may be a fitting place for our worship of our Lady and our Lord. So be it done.

Carrying a candle:

> With the hot flame of desire I do cleanse, consecrate and bless this circle that it may be a fitting place for our worship of our Lady and our Lord. So be it done.

Carrying a bowl of water, sprinkling as you go:

> With the flowing waters breath of love I do cleanse, consecrate and bless this circle that it may be a fitting place for our worship of our Lady and our Lord. So be it done.

Carrying a bowl of soil, sprinkling as you go:

> With the fertile earth of wisdom I do cleanse, consecrate and bless this circle that it may be a fitting place for our worship of our Lady and our Lord. So be it done.

ASPURGENCES FOR PREGNANCY OR
BIRTHING RITUALS

Sweet air of life, first breath of newborn lungs, blow forth in this place and create a place of learning.

Bright fire of lust, first cry of the newborn babe, burn forth in this place and create a place of desire.

Gushing waters of birth, first cradle of the babe, flow forth in this place and create a place of love.

Earth breast of the Mother, first provider for the child, stand firm and full in this place and nourish its stability.

CALLING OF THE GUARDIANS

I summon, stir, and call thee up, o ye mighty ones of the East, to guard this circle and witness this rite and bless that working I work this night.

I summon, stir, and call thee up, o ye mighty ones of the South, to guard this circle and witness this rite and bless that working I work this night.

I summon, stir, and call thee up, o ye mighty ones of the West, to guard this circle and witness this rite and bless that working I work this night.

I summon, stir, and call thee up, o ye mighty ones of the North, to guard this circle and witness this rite and bless that working I work this night.

CALL TO THE GODDESS

This is the call by the leader or the group to the Goddess, asking her to send her energy and her caring to the group, the gathering, and the work to be done.

I will sing of well-founded Earth, Mother of All, Eldest of Things. You feed all creatures that are in the world, all that go lightly upon the goodly lands, all that are in the paths of the seas, all that fly across the skies; all are fed of Your store. Through you, O Lady, are women and men blessed in their children and their harvests; to You it belongs to take these things away. Happy are we, Your children, whom You delight to bless; full are our spirits, our souls and our lives. O Holy Goddess, Great Moon Mother, thus it is that we call out unto You to visit us with Your presence, Your wisdom and Your blessing.

GOD INVOCATION

This is a call to the Lady's Consort, the Lord of the Dance and the Hunt. This may be left out if that is the will of your group.

I will sing of the wild things, children of our Father, lover and beloved of Her. You are the fire of life that lives in all creatures that are in the world, all that go lightly upon the goodly lands, all that are in the paths of the seas, all that fly across the skies; all these burn with Your fire. Through you, O beloved of Her, are men and women blessed in their children and their harvests; to You it belongs to give joy and desire and knowledge of the Dance of Life. Happy is the person whom You delight to honor; fertile the fields you plow, round the bellies you fill. Happy are we, beloved of Her, Your children, whom You delight to bless. O Great Consort, thus it is that we call out unto You to visit us with Your presence, Your wisdom and Your blessing.

WORKING

Now is the time set aside for your private or group worship, meditation and magickal working.

FAREWELL TO THE GODDESS

This follows the working, and is the group's thanks for the attendance and assistance of the Goddess.

Great Lady, Goddess who is the Earth itself, provider for Her children, we have called and You have come forth and witnessed our love, respect and worship for you. For this and for all other gifts, both known and unknown, we thank You and bid You hail and farewell.

FAREWELL TO THE GOD

If the Consort was called then He, too, should be thanked for His presence and aid.

> Consort of our Lady, lover and beloved of Her, Teacher of the Dance of Life, we have called and You have come forth and witnessed our love, respect and worship for You. For this and for all other gifts, both known and unknown, we thank You and bid You hail and farewell.

FAREWELL TO THE GUARDIANS

Here the elemental forces which have been called are now thanked and dismissed.

> I have summoned, stirred, and called thee up, o ye mighty ones of the North, and you have come and guarded this circle and witnessed this rite and blessed the working; now, ere ye depart for your wondrous realm I bid ye Hail and Farewell.

> I have summoned, stirred, and called thee up, o ye mighty ones of the West, and you have come and guarded this circle and witnessed this rite and blessed the working; now, ere ye depart for your wondrous realm I bid ye Hail and Farewell.

> I have summoned, stirred, and called thee up, o ye mighty ones of the South, and you have come and guarded this circle and witnessed this rite and blessed the working; now, ere ye depart for your wondrous realm I bid ye Hail and Farewell.

> I have summoned, stirred, and called thee up, o ye mighty ones of the East, and you have come and guarded this circle and witnessed this rite and blessed the working; now, ere ye depart for your wondrous realm I bid ye Hail and Farewell.

CLOSING THE CIRCLE

The circle is erased by retracing it, this time in a counterclockwise direction, or "widdershins," drawing the energy into a

candle carried by the person banishing the circle. When the process is complete, this person blows out the candle and immediately stomps on the ground, grounding the energy into the earth.

This circle is now open, go in beauty and in love.

Chapter 12
Full Body Art

There are a few simple suggestions which should be followed before actually decorating yourself or someone else.

First, decide what you want to accomplish with a design before you begin to apply it. Use meditation and counselling to be as sure as possible that what you intend is the best possible thing, given the situation. If you are working with someone else, ascertain that they agree with you.

Then, knowing what you want to accomplish and being certain that your action is the best possible one, decide which tools you will use and how you will use them to achieve the optimum effect. Take a few minutes to consider your materials. Compare symbols, analyze colors, decide on the use of scents. You want the strongest possible result in the shortest possible time, so maximize the strengths of your tools. Remember, prior to the ritual, test your materials on all your subjects for adverse reactions.

Ask yourself how easily the color can be removed after your ritual. Several years ago a friend asked if it would be possible for me to paint her in such a way that she would regain her fertility. Of course it was possible, and I proceeded. How was I to know that the particular green I used was nearly impossible to remove? Imagine her embarrassment when, four days later, on a visit to her doctor, he asked about the green tinge covering her entire abdomen! Magic is a wonderful thing. But even with magic, there is a place (several times over) for practicality. However, do not be too cautious. If the colors come off too easily, they may disappear during your ritual and be ineffective.

The Designs

Now, let's see what some of these large designs look like when they're applied. Several of the designs are illustrated in the picture section.

FEMALE COMING OF AGE

One design that I created was for the celebratory painting of a young woman about to be taken into her "First Blood" or menarche ritual, welcoming her into the community of adult women in a Women's Mysteries group. The symbols would represent Woman, Protection, Wisdom and Strength, all in blood red.

The vertical red line from the top of her head to the pubic triangle is a bloodline, representing her lineage and the potential lineage through her. At this particular ritual, the young woman's mother would also wear a central bloodline, as would her grandmother. Other blood relatives might choose to be similarly marked, but on their bodies the red line would be off-center.

Once the bloodline is placed, it is covered in the lower sternum and upper abdominal area with the symbol of Goddess Invocation in white or, secondarily, blue. The symbol of the horned moon, representing the Goddess and the horns of the womb could be used here.

The green triangle, outlined in red, demonstrates this woman's newly gained Fertility, wrapped, as it were, in her menstrual blood. Within this triangle, one of the several symbols for Flow can be placed to insure regular menses. This combination of colors and symbols represents a number of different concepts. The first is the desire, on the part of the group, for regular menses and fertility on the part of the subject. It is also a lesson in the meaning of menstruation, dramatically demonstrating to the subject her new biological capacity for childbearing. Other symbols might be added by the women at the ceremony, signifying specific attributes that they wish to invoke in the subject, and involving themselves in her life. See photograph 1.

In addition to these symbols, the sigil for Physical Strength can be added to the young woman's back. Black is used to increase her strength should she need it for work, childbearing, and other tasks. If the sigil is outlined in white, it would represent bone and would help to prevent osteoporosis. See photograph 3.

MALE RITE OF PASSAGE

For a young man's rite of passage into adulthood the design would include a white face to signify that he had 'died.' Black bands on the arms and legs would be used to signify physical strength, and axes would demonstrate the rebirth of the body. The symbols of Bodily Change in this design are much more important for the male than the female, because the female, with her menarche, has physical proof of her bodily changes. Here, again, the bloodline is applied, extending from the crown of the head to the phallus, teaching the boy that he is now sexually mature and must take responsibility for his sexual activities.

On his chest are the Male triangle as well as the sigils for Strength, Perseverance and Wisdom, all in red. A rear view would show that a second symbol for Physical Strength, the traditional "lazy E," has been added to his back. Another sigil that would be appropriate here would be Change, the passing of the individual through a barrier, added either to the chest or to the abdomen, again in red.

FERTILITY

Male

The basic fertility design for a man is quite simple in that it is the combination of three basic symbols. The first, of course, is the bloodline coming down from the crown over the torso. However, for those who object to having paint applied to their face, the line may begin at the throat. This starting point is also used when a mask is being worn. The second symbol is one which draws upon the fertility of the earth and carries it up from the feet, over the legs, to the abdomen, where it joins the lifeline. These two symbols join together and form a third symbol, that for male Sexuality and Potency, a prong raised above the horizontal, symbolic of the enlarged phallus. See photograph 2.

Female

A design similar to the Female Coming of Age may be applied to a woman who wishes to conceive. The green lozenge, depicted in photograph 4, is outlined in red with red perpendicular lines connecting the sides; this symbol represents the plowed field. The red dots in the center of each of the four smaller lozenges thus constructed represent the seeds planted in that field. The color red is used to illustrate the spark of life. The symbol for Physical Strength can be added along each forearm.

Once again, the bloodline is used. Lines running up each of the legs draw upon the fertility of the earth and carry it up from the feet, over the legs to join the lifeline. A number of symbols can be applied to the lifeline, including a compound symbol constructed of the signs for Pregnancy and Wisdom, along with one asking the blessing of, or possession by, the Goddess. In the area of the sternum another compound symbol may be added composed of Prayer and Happiness.

The white chevrons above each breast, the symbol for Provision or More, are to ensure an ample supply of milk (white) for her child. A symbol meaning Perseverance can be placed just above and between the chevrons to help the subject persevere in her attempts to become pregnant and to prevent discouragement. Other symbols might have been added here such as those for Physical Strength, Wisdom, and Love.

PREGNANCY

Designs can be created for the trimesters. The first trimester ritual celebrates and magically reinforces the pregnancy. The design builds on the Fertility pattern used to achieve pregnancy by adding the Goddess Invocation in white, outlined in red. The energy of the Goddess (white), wrapped in life force (red), is being drawn down into and around the fertile, plowed and seeded field. The only change in the lozenge is that a fifth red point is added to the center of the symbol. See photographs 5 and 6 for variations.

In a design for the second trimester, the Goddess sigil is used twice. The second symbol, replacing the lozenge, represents a prayer for the Goddess's help in carrying the child through this difficult trimester and a dedication of the life being carried to the way of the Goddess. The fifth dot representing New Life is replaced by the Birth sigil. See photographs 7 and 8 for variations.

The third trimester ritual also uses a Goddess Invocation symbol on the forehead, in white outlined in red or black, leading down to a white or blue filled circle on the abdomen. The sphere is decorated with one or more (depending on the number of children being carried) green life symbols outlined in red or red life symbols outlined in black. The womb, filled with the blue waters of life or reflective of the full moon of the Mother Goddess, is the home of the fetus. When the life symbol is outlined in red it shows new life surrounded with energy. When in red outlined in black it reflects life energy outlined with strength. See photograph 9.

BIRTHING

Direct

A design for birthing is applied directly to the mother-to-be in order to strengthen her and to ease her delivery. The symbols here are strong and simple. The bloodline should be used but, once again, may be deleted if the subject objects to paint on the face. A red Spiral of Life is painted on the abdomen. The spiral has nine rounds, one for each month of the pregnancy. If this were an early delivery, a smaller number of rounds would be used. On the breasts, once again, the blue or white symbols for Provision or Increase are used, unless the mother would not be nursing her child. Between these chevrons is the symbol for Perseverance, this time in emotional blue and quite large. On the forehead can be placed the Prayer or Invocation sigil in white, asking the help, guidance and blessings of the Goddess, or the Meditation or Wisdom symbol in blue. On the thighs are the markings for Decrease of Flow, in red, to prevent hemorrhage or unnecessary bleeding during childbirth.

On her back, the woman would have the sigil for Physical Strength in black, with the base of the sigil quite low and running well up the length of the spine and the sides. Some women add black, brown or green lines from the soles of their feet up to the base of the Strength symbol, drawing the strength of the Earth into them for this event.

Care must be taken with this particular decoration. None of the paint should interfere with the birthing. The paint used on the abdomen should be one that can be removed quickly and completely should there be a complication with the delivery and a Caesarian delivery become necessary. See photograph 10.

Indirect

As an alternative in situations when it would be inappropriate or impossible to place the preceding design directly on the birthing woman or in situations when a support group wishes to send energy to the birthing mother, a similar design is applied to a priestess or energy channel, who will serve as the focus for sending this energy. Basically, this is the same decoration as is used on the mother with a few changes. Instead of a perfect spiral on the abdomen, this spiral is pear-shaped, creating a bit of an optical illusion and making the priestess appear pregnant. The chevrons of Provision are used to focus the will and create the illusion of enlargement and distention. It is good to use such illusions on the substitute focus so that more energy is applied to the work rather than wasted on visualization. This can go as far as making the channel up to appear as much like the focal person as is possible, including the use of wigs and other props.

As with the design for the mother-to-be, the symbols for Goddess Invocation, Perseverance and Strength are appropriate. However, since the child to be born is not that of the channel, the bloodline is not used. See photograph 11.

ADOPTION

Female

The basic pattern for adoption includes the bloodline, the symbol for Family, and the Invocation/Evocation of Deity. The details in how these symbols are applied and combined are of utmost importance.

For an adopting parent, the bloodline does not begin at the crown but, rather, comes from the top of the shoulder; the right shoulder in the case of the adopting father and the left for the adopting mother. This shows that, while there is continuity of family, it is not via birth. The line extends from the appropriate shoulder, across to the line of invocation, where it turns downward and leads directly to, and joins, the symbol for family.

The symbol for the Goddess in her mother aspect, the full moon, is applied to the brow of the adopting mother, and a vertical line of white then continues downward to where the

blue Family symbol has been applied over the center of the
chest. In its progress downward, it meets and surrounds the red
lifeline, bringing divine guidance and support to surround the
creation of family. There the line is expanded into a filled
white circle that envelopes the family.

Male

For the adoptive father, the warm, nurturing sun is applied in
bright yellow on the brow. A yellow line then drops to the
Family symbol, again in blue, and joins with or surrounds that
symbol, changing and blending parts of it to green, indicative
of his desire to help nurture the family and see it grow. As with
the adoptive mother, the vertical yellow line joins with, and
reinforces, the lifeline, guiding it toward the creation of true
family. See photograph 12.

MOURNING

Miscarriage

Designs can also be created to assist the ritual mourning process of a woman who has miscarried or undergone an abortion.
This set of symbols begins with a lifeline that goes from the
top of the head to the womb. Surrounding the bottom end of
that line is a green lozenge, to insure the Fertility of the
woman. Below this, directly over the internal sexual organs, is
the alternate symbol for Strength in its healing aspect. The
blue decreasing tears placed on her cheeks aid the woman in
mourning and remind her that grief eventually lessens, allowing the memory to be kept with love. Finally, the sigil to
prevent hemorrhage is added to the thighs. See photographs 13
and 14 for variations.

Abortion

If the mourning ritual is done in conjunction with an abortion,
additional symbols are added to the miscarriage design. These
include painting the left hand with the red of blood, assisting
the woman to accept her personal responsibility for the abor-

tion, and the black labrys, which is symbolic of Rebirth. The latter symbol is placed on the solar plexus to teach the woman that the soul of the fetus will be reborn yet again, relieving her of unnecessary guilt. See photograph 15.

CRONING

Designs can be created for painting a woman for her croning ritual, the celebration of her loss of fertility and entrance into the community of elders. The essential symbols for this work are the bloodline, ending over the womb and culminating in a triple lunar symbol with a black, dark moon at the center. At the upper end of the bloodline is the symbol for Wisdom; on the sternum is a sigil for Strength, and over the solar plexus is a symbol for the Invocation of the Goddess. These are, respectively, red, red and white.

DEATH

The design for the body of a soul that has passed would focus around a large black labrys, symbolic of Death and Rebirth, covering nearly the entire chest. Applied to the labrys will be sigils to invoke the Goddess and the God, the Goddess sigil in white on the left breast, and the God sigil in yellow on the right. Family and friends may add other symbols as they feel appropriate. See photograph 16.

INITIATION

For a young man or woman on a journey of spiritual discovery or initiation, the face would be white to indicate the state of "otherness," detachment from the profane world. A black band across the mouth and face tells others that they should refrain from interrupting the journey and that, any words the initiate speaks will not be his or her own but, rather, thoughts and energies channelled from the "other" world.

HANDFASTING

An appropriate design could be created for celebrating Hand-fasting (marriage) skyclad. The skyclad tradition is based on the belief that the couple should enter this ritual naked to one another, giving to one another without reservation, revealed to their spouse-to-be and to the community as a whole.

The woman may be marked with the red symbol of Sexual Union or with an unusual fertility symbol, resembling her upper reproductive tract. This symbol is usually applied in green. Red dots equal to the number of children she wishes to have are applied around this symbol. These symbols indicate her level of comfort with her own sexuality and her desire to conceive and bear children.

Her right hand, the hand that will be bound to her spouse's, is colored red to indicate her willingness to share her life with him. Likewise, his left hand is red and he also wears symbols for Sexual Union and Fertility.

At the time of the Handfasting ritual other symbols will be added by the priestess and priest presiding. As an alternative to the more traditional pricking and sharing of blood, these two will be marked with the hexagram in white, on the backs of their joined hands to mark the moment of wedding. Well-wishers will then be free to add such symbols as they desire, usually those of Strength, Perseverance, Protection, Wealth, Health and, if desired by the couple, Children.

Another context for such magick would be during a shower-like betrothal, where the women celebrate separately from the men, and vice-versa. In this context the symbols can be quite large, bright and of a teasing nature. But remember, what you depict is what you want to happen—this is not just a game. See photographs 17 and 18.

HANDPARTING

If Handfasting is a spiritual ritual, then so too is Handparting, or separation. Unfortunately, such a ritual is rarely celebrated by the two parties. Should they do so, it goes far in healing the emotional scars, especially when this is done before their spiritual community. For this ritual the colors and symbols are

the blue of tears, the white of non-involvement on the hands and, added at the end of the ceremony by the community, the symbols of Love, Acceptance and Strength. The addition of symbols by the community is very important because it demonstrates to both people that they have the support of their friends, that the people around them refuse to choose between them and will remain loyal to both.

DEDICATION BY THE ELEMENTS

Body painting would be most powerful for an individual preparing to enter into a ritual introducing her/himself to the elements and seeking balance and power via Air, Fire, Water and Earth. Air and Fire have traditionally been seen as male elements, Water and Earth, female. Each pattern, with some alterations however, would be appropriate on a person of either sex.

Air

Air ritual colors traditionally associated with that magical element are yellow, gray and purple. Yellow appeals to the bright properties of Air: imagination, intellect and clear-headedness. Gray strikes the more hidden aspects: analysis, concentration and investigation. Finally, purple appeals to the spiritual part of Air: the gift of communication and the broadness of vision. The large area of yellow on the face is compensated by purple on the mouth and the ears (communication consisting of both speaking and listening). The symbols for strength and perseverance are gray, while gray on the feet serves to keep the wearer firmly planted in the earth as his mind floats among the stars.

This is a basic design. The proportions of the colors can be altered, depending on the personality of the person entering into the elemental ritual. The more practical and analytical the person is, the more yellow there should be. The more imaginative the person, the more gray. The same holds true for purple: one who talks much and listens little will have both sides of the head covered in purple with very little applied to the mouth, while a shy, introverted or withdrawn person would likely have the reverse.

Fire

For a Fire ritual, the face, hands and feet are all painted red, as are a Wisdom triangle on the abdomen and a Strength symbol on the chest. The wearer is to become Fire: to touch with the touch of Fire, to walk upon feet of Fire, to learn of Fire as creator and destroyer. This is why neither of the two supplemental colors of Fire (orange and yellow-white) are included. Similarly to the individual adjustments for Air, the amount of red must depend on the temperament of the person involved. Here caution must be exercised to a greater degree. You cannot take a person who is not very fiery and simply use a lot of red. That would be like trying to bake a better cake by turning the oven up to 500 degrees. The key with a person who is not very fiery is to start with as much red as the person has Fire, then add just a little more. The same holds true for a person with a fiery temperament. Through such an application, the ritual will help them learn the true nature of Fire and be burned clean and pure by it.

Water

A woman preparing for her Water ritual would be painted with blues and blue-greens to represent the flow of cleansing Water through the wearer. The central focus of this particular design is the blue, point-down triangle on the abdomen which covers the triangle formed between the pubis and the two points of her hips. A male would have the same mark, but much smaller. From this triangle, Water flows down to the earth; from it rises a fountain bringing fertile, cleansing, female Water up over the face and the brow. Droplets fall down to the breasts. From this fountain as well, healing flows down the arms and over the fingers. As well as having a much smaller triangle, the male would have less fountain splash to the forehead, though the lines down the arms and legs would be proportional.

Earth

For an Earth ritual it is important, as it was for Air, to use a variety of the colors of Earth; the black with its strength of mountains, brown representing the fertility of the Earth, and green to bring life into being. No one color could possibly impart all of the lessons of Earth by itself.

The design starts with lines of all three colors rising from the soles of the feet, out of the Earth itself. Dual black lines come together above the buttocks and, joined, rise up the spine, bringing strength of body and of character. Green, illustrating life and, to some extent, openness, rises from the feet to cover the face. This prevents the black from becoming overpowering and making the person inflexible. Green also extends down the arms, bringing the magic of life and growth to the hands that will tend the fields, aid their fellows, and heal the sick. The fertility of brown rises from the feet to the reproductive organs to bring fertility. Brown also rises to the heart, making it fertile, and a good place for love, kindness and under-standing to grow.

DIVINE INVOCATION

The Goddess as the Prime Female Force

A priestess preparing to invoke the Goddess has her face painted turquoise, the essential female color. This removes the ego and opens the way to her essential femaleness. A Prayer/-Supplication symbol begins directly above her womb and ex-tends upward to the solar plexus, where it branches upward and outward over the breasts. Thus, the essential core of her femaleness, the center of her being and the sources of nourish-ment for new life, all take part in this prayer.

Answering that prayer is the symbol to Invoke the Goddess, this time in its full phase, a white disc on the forehead. This energy is then channeled downwards, over the third eye, over the lips, over the throat and vocal cords to the sternum, where it splits and spreads to meet and join with the Prayer. Both the

Prayer and the Invocation can be in the white of the Moon, indicating a particular type of invocation that is sought, just as does the particular Moon symbol on the forehead. All of the white lines can be outlined in black, strengthening the resolve and sense of purpose this woman takes into her ritual. See photograph 19.

The Goddess as the Lady of the Moon

This design is utilized when invoking the more nurturing Mother aspect of the Goddess, preferably in rituals coinciding with the full moon itself. For this design, most of the segments are the same as the Goddess as the Prime Female Force. The primary difference is that the face is painted white, perhaps outlined in either black or dark blue. The line downward from the face may also continue the theme of night outlining the moon, perhaps going so far as to extend over the full body of the woman.

The supplication or prayer symbol in this case can be in red, indicative of life; white, the color of openness and receptivity; the brown or green of the earth or fields; or the woman's personal color. See photograph 20.

Invoking the God

A priest invoking the Old God, Saturn or Pluto, has his face painted black except for the lips which are painted red to indicate he will communicate with others. An orange Male triangle is added to his chest. The right hand, the male hand, is painted orange as well. To balance this, the left hand is colored turquoise.

HIEROS GAMOS

One of the most sacred Pagan rites is the Hieros Gamos, the Sacred Marriage or Great Rite. It represents the joining together of the Goddess and the God in the forms of the priestess and the priest. The symbols used therefore are among the very oldest and most powerful.

Female

The woman wears the black of fertility and the red of blood in the ancient symbol for female Sexual Acceptance and desire. The symbol is superimposed over the entire torso in a way that enfolds the body while emphasizing sexuality. The neck of this symbol extends upwards to surround the face, which may be colored white to represent the Goddess in Her Full Moon/-Mother aspect or Her New Moon/Maiden aspect, or turquoise to represent femaleness as a whole, what Hindus call Shakti. The painting of the face is done, once again, to push the individual ego aside in order to allow the woman so painted to become a vessel for a far greater force. See photograph 23.

Male

The primary male symbol—the tree—can be joined by Strength or other symbols as appropriate. The design may be portrayed in two very different sets of colors. The first is green outlined in black (or white) which combines the representation of the male sexual principle with the symbol for strength, thus creating a synergistic combination representative of the tree as the strong center pole of the world. Again, the symbol extends upward to frame the face, colored white, green or orange, and may extend outward to the shoulders and down the arms, indicating the male role as protector. This also gives physical strength to the entire body. Such a design is usually used when it is the desire of the female participant to conceive a child during the ritual. See photographs 21 and 22.

The alternative keeps this strong symbol combination but changes the color at the heart of the design from green and orange or white, to red. This alternative is used when the focus of the rite is power or joyous celebration, rather than conception or fertility. See photograph 24.

HEALING

I was recently approached to assist in the emotional healing of a 17-year-old woman who had been raped at the age of 5. She

144

had suppressed all memories of the event but, at the age of 15 had been told about the event due to emotional problems she began to suffer. Two years of therapy had little effect and I was approached in a last-ditch attempt to heal her through ritual. The effective design I created was as follows:

1. A blue Wisdom triangle on the forehead, filled with the Moon outlined in black to combine emotion with wisdom and invoke the Dark Goddess.

2. Black stripes down her arms, legs and along her trunk to give strength. These lines were to integrate her physically, mentally and spiritually and help her focus on her body which she was reluctant to do.

3. A red Strength "E" on her back, applied over a black Fear symbol to encourage her to conquer her fear.

4. One, then two, then one tears on her cheeks, in blue to activate and then release the mourning process.

5. Yellow around her mouth, outlined in red, to speak honestly, with passion and to release the anger there.

6. A red flame at her center encircled by a full Moon, surrounded by a protection symbol in yellow/gold. The flame represents her life force contained and protected by the Goddess as Moon. The yellow/gold represents a new aura surrounding her.

7. A blue triple wave Flow symbol between her breasts to allow the emotions to flow.

Chapter 13
Sabbats, Esbats
and the Elements

I can attest to the truth of a "shared reality" and the magickal strength of such a reality when enough energy is put into it. A group of people, holding an ideal and working in concert, can create an alternate, subjectively-shared reality for a period of time. This is sacred time and space.

Alternate realities are described by Michael Harner, Carlos Castenada, and Mircea Eliade in their works on shamanistic practices and Voudoun or Macumba rituals (where props and costumes are regularly provided for the loas). I would imagine that such a state of alternate reality was created during the rituals of the medieval witches, who claimed to fly on animals or broomsticks to far places, there to take part in fantastic rituals. Various herbal substances were probably used to induce this state and props were doubtlessly used by the leaders to add credibility.

Unfortunately, shared reality can have a shadow or negative side. Many of us know people who focus so much time and energy on fantasy worlds or role playing games and are so wrapped up in their creation that they will not or cannot cope with the mundane world. Another negative example of shared reality was created by Reverend Jim Jones in Jonestown. This reality became so overpowering, partially due to the isolation of this group, that people willingly committed suicide or allowed the murder of those unwilling to die voluntarily.

A healthy shared reality is created only for a time, and when that time is over the energy is grounded and you must again walk in the mundane world. With that understanding, shared reality is not dangerous. It is a powerful magickal tool that can be used for worship or to alter the world around you.

When working in a group, ritual body art can be created three ways. The first is where each person applies her/his own art, an opportunity for personal experience and self-expression. The second calls for each member to apply ritual art to one other person, thus promoting a sharing experience as well as creative expression. Finally, one person can decorate the entire group, promoting a focusing dynamic. Decoration, whether done individually, co-operatively or as a group, not only helps you draw closer to the object of your working, it also helps to bring the group closer together through the physical, emotional and spiritual contact brought about by the art.

Simple Art

If you're doing a ritual on the night of the full Moon, use a black or dark blue pencil to draw a circle on your forehead, then fill in the circle with white grease paint. This can be done before or as part of the ritual itself to bring you closer to the lunar energy of the night. A ritual done on the night of the new Moon can be treated in exactly the same way, but with the colors reversed: a white outline first, filled in with black. For rituals done during the waxing and waning of the Moon, harmonize with the lunar cycle by creating the partial disc you desire with black, then filling it with white.

Equally simple are makeup schemes for rituals which focus on the primal elements. For Air, the primary color would be yellow, supplemented with pale violets and grays. For Fire the primary color would, of course, be red, supplemented by orange and yellow-white. Water is based on various blues, with turquoise or aquamarine and blue-violet highlights. Finally, for an Earth ritual you would use browns and greens with some black, possibly for highlighting or dividing.

Many body art rituals focus primarily on the face, but the area can be extended as far as you wish. Full-body makeup is more than just decoration; it is a tool for the alteration of consciousness as well as for magick. A few years ago I was decorated in a joint project by more than a dozen people who had been models during one of my seminars. They prepared me to attend the main ritual at a major midwestern Pagan festival by covering me from head to toe in brown grease paint. Not satisfied with this, a thin, irregular coat of moss green was added. Finally, to top things off, a pair of horns were applied to my forehead using eyelash cement. All of this served to create a rather interesting and fairly authentic Pan-like look.

If you wish to extend the makeup for lunar rituals to cover the face or an even larger area, you may want to color the entire area blue-black, then add stars. Taken to the extreme, the entire body being colored, you would find yourself made up as the ancient Egyptians visualized the goddess Nut.

Designs can be used for celebration and to work magic on the sacred Pagan holidays. Samhain, October 31, marks the night when the curtain between the planes is at its thinnest. It is a night of divination and celebration of death. A good place to begin is with a bright face swathed in dark cloth or a black face. A face painted black brings the consciousness of the wearer into contact with that sense of otherness that permeates Samhain. To the black can be added a symbol to Invoke the Goddess or God and a white band across the mouth indicating a readiness to act as a voice for the Gods or for the dead. The eyelids can be painted to resemble eyes, showing that the wearer has the ability to see both the visible and the invisible.

For women or Goddess-oriented men, the wearer is made up to look as beautiful, as attractive and as desirable as possible, but this beauty is then hidden behind a black veil. This reflects the beauty of the Goddess, hiding behind the veil of death. In many ways this treatment reflects the story of Persephone, gone to the underworld to learn the secret of death, whose beauty makes her a slave of the Dark Lord.

Next around the circle comes Yule on the Winter Equinox. For the crown of lights of the Saint Lucia celebration (borrowed by Christians from an earlier Pagan celebration), a young woman, usually the youngest daughter, wears a chaplet of holly and mistletoe and bearing eight candles, one for each Sabbat. Through the use of very pale skin colors with stark lips and eyes, women in their Mother aspect bring to life the Snow Queen, White Lady of the Snows. The effect can be enhanced through the use of silver sparkle around the eyes, lightly over the face, and in the hair. A male counterpart to this is the Sun King, which combines the use of a gold or yellow solar mask with the solar signs on the palms of both hands, also in gold or yellow. If you don't have access to such a mask, gold face and hair coloring make an acceptable substitute.

Imbolc, or Candlemas, February 2, is a time devoted to the family and, most especially, to daughters and younger women. A girl prepared for Imbolc would be robed in the white of winter, made up to be as beautiful and mature as possible, and crowned with a chaplet or wreath of lights. She brings light to the family and awakens them physically and spiritually, the promise she holds reflecting the promise of the new life to come in the approaching Spring.

Eostre, the Vernal Equinox, is easy to celebrate. The colors are obvious: gold and purple and, to a lesser degree, the other colors of early spring blossoms, with lots of flowers, ribbons and other items that display the bright promise of Spring. Young people are decorated with white or blue faces with a yellow circle on the forehead, depicting the warmth and bright sunlight soon to come. The hard boiled egg, sliced and served either plain or deviled, also represents the new, warm sun

shining through the fast fading clouds of winter. When the yolk is removed you can soak the cooked white in blue food coloring, then restore the bright yellow yolk, a sun face in a blue sky.

For Beltane, May 1, nearly anything bright, playful, and/or attractive is allowed, even expected. Ritual clothing at this time of year tends to be revealing, so the addition of some makeup or body design really helps to set the mood. Perhaps, in celebration of the time of year, a man or woman will choose to cover his/her legs with vines or flowers, real, artificial or painted. Small horns, real or artificial, help create the atmosphere as well. Crowns and garlands of bright flowers are common, and makeup is appropriate for either sex, especially when it draws attention to the eyes.

Lithia, the Summer Solstice, is the time when the brightest and hottest colors are seen; vibrant oranges, startling yellows and life-filled greens. Lithia is the time for a celebration of the strength, speed and courage of all the young people of the community. It is also often a time to test the younger members of the community prior to granting recognition or privileges.

Smaller bits of body art focus on solar discs in yellow or gold on the forehead, hands or both. One other bit of decoration you may want to create for Lithia are crowns of laurel, real or imitation or even of brass or other golden metal. These are awarded to the winners of the games and contests often held to celebrate this festival.

Lammas, celebrated on August 1, is the time for reds, especially the slightly darker shades. Lammas is the old summer Fire Festival and often celebrates the defeat of youth and strength by time and age. Lammas focuses on the young men, in that it marks an end to their freedom and the assumption of their responsibilities toward their community, thus balancing the celebration of young women held at Imbolc.

A mystery play often performed at this time focuses on the

defeat of the Young God by his darker, older self, the God of the Underworld. This is symbolized in the use of reds, reflecting the blood shed by the Young God. Another way of showing this is the application of drops of red to the hands or the face, either before or during the play. Oak wreaths and holly wreaths can be worn by the men, based on their age. Women wear mistletoe or roses because, while male life may come and go, femaleness is eternal.

Finally, we come to Mabon, the Autumnal Equinox. All the Earth colors come out with a passion: the browns, golds, yellows, oranges and red of the field and the forest. Also seen on some of the young men are the dark green of the evergreens. A common treatment for faces is to cover the forehead with brown and then add the symbol of the individual with the raised arms of Prayer, in this case, of Thanksgiving. An alternative would be to color the bottom half of the forehead brown and add a symbol for Life or Promise, such as an oval representing a grain with a dot of red at its center. Then, directly above the brown, add a symbol for harvest or a wheat sheaf.

Chaplets are especially common at Mabon, depicting the various gifts of the Goddess to Her people. These can be decorated with flowers, fruit and vegetables. If you make a wreath exclusively of real items, you can use it also as an offering to the Earth and a treat to the many creatures with which we share it. After it has fulfilled its purpose, take it out and hang it from a tree at the ritual site or at your home.

Chapter 14
Everyday Use of Ritual Body Art

So, all the symbols have wonderful meaning and will help your ritual experience, but what about the other 700 or more hours of every month? What else can this magic do? The only limit to what you can accomplish with these techniques is your own imagination.

For example, at one time I engaged in full-contact, armed martial arts. In one bout I forgot a piece of protective gear designed to prevent injury to my forearm. Needless to say, that is exactly where I got hit, resulting in a broken bone. After a cast was put on, I drew the broken bone on the cast and, each day, drew the ends of the bone closer together. After I had the ends joined, I continued drawing each day, making the join stronger and reinforcing the areas near the break. The result: I had the cast off in four weeks and the X-ray showed that I had healed cleanly and completely. The drawing served to help me to visualize and, thus speed up the healing process.

Do you suffer from depression? A common term for this is to say that you are "under a cloud." Take a few minutes every day to paint or draw a dark cloud on your forehead. Then, when you can really see that cloud, either slowly and ritualistically wash it away—or paint a bright, happy sun over it! Try this for a month and see if your mood changes. But you do have to set aside some time for this each and every day, no excuses allowed.

How about you who are shy, afraid to open your mouths when others are around? What might happen if, every day for a month, you applied a black band across your mouth and lower face for an hour or so? Of course, you would have to remain silent. And what if each day that band was narrower and narrower until, at the end of the month, there was no band at all? You would feel much more free to express yourself. If, along the way you applied yellow in ever greater expanses to your face, starting with only a small dot in the center of your forehead, you might be surprised by how intelligent and witty a conversationalist you turn out to be.

Do you have an energy blockage somewhere in your body? Reconnect the break with red lines. For inflammations, swelling and pain, use a thin, cold wash of ice blue across the affected area. For general soreness, brush inward with light strokes toward the center of the area, using red paint.

Do you find yourself unable to study or concentrate, or do you suffer from writer's block? An air symbol, in yellow, applied to the forehead, combined with a little meditation or quiet time usually does the trick.

For times when you need extra energy to get through a project or are faced with seemingly insurmountable odds, try using a little energy-producing orange as a small symbol on your heart if possible. If you can't do that, then add the orange to your wardrobe.

This brings up a new point: the combination of colors and symbols in your wardrobe. You would be amazed how successfully you can decorate a few accessories such as scarves, ties and belts with colors and symbols, using something as simple as a potato. Cut a potato in half, then carve a symbol, removing all but that symbol. You're now ready to block print garments, accessories or even cards, using ink or paint. If you don't want to go to that length, use permanent fabric markers in a variety of colors. Finally, for those of you with patience, there's the elegance of embroidery. Because of the amount of energy, concentration and effort involved, this is the most powerful of these techniques.

If you're trying to deal with a situation that arises half-way through your work day and you really can't find the time to apply the symbols, colors and/or scents on the physical plane, apply them with your imagination. Visualize them so totally and completely that you actually begin to feel them on your skin. Just because other people can't see the colors and designs doesn't make them any less effective. Making your visualizations strong and alive can only be achieved through practice.

The only limits, as I have said, will be those of your own imagination. Take a moment to consider any situation. Break it down into its simplest components. Then take each one and look at it in the context of colors and their meanings. Alternatively, look to the symbols that would be most appropriate for your situation.

Now, it's all up to you. Start your own experiments with color and how they affect you. Begin to create your own lexicon of symbols. And, more importantly, share your thoughts and ideas with others who, like you, choose to add this powerful tool to their magickal repertoire.

Sources

Alloway, Laurence and Carolee Schneemann. "The Body as Object and Instrument," *Art in America*. March, 1980.

Artist's Color Wheel. The Color Wheel Co., 1989.

Beck, Renee and Sydney Barbara Metrick. *The Art of the Round: A Guide to Creating and Performing Your Own Rituals for Growth and Change.* Berkeley: Celestial Arts, 1990.

Berger, Pamela. *The Goddess Obscured.* Boston: Beacon Press, 1985.

Blum, Ralph. *The Book of Runes.* New York: St. Martin's Press, 1982.

Boone, Elizabeth H. *The Codex Magliabechiano and the Lost Prototype of the Magliabechiano Group.* Berkeley: University of California Press, 1983.

Buckland, Raymond. *Buckland's Complete Book of Witchcraft.* Minneapolis: Llewellyn Publishing, 1987.

———. *Practical Color Magick.* Minneapolis: Llewellyn Publishing, 1983.

Budapest, Zsuzsanna E. *The Holy Book of Women's Mysteries.* 2nd ed. Berkeley: Wingbow Press, 1989.

Bunzel, Ruth. "Introduction to Zuni Ceremonialism," *Bureau of American Ethnology*. 47th Annual Report. Washington, D.C.: Smithsonian Institution, 1929–30.

Caitlin, George. *O-Kee-Pa.* New Haven: Yale University Press, 1967.

Calverley, Roger. A. *The Healing Gems.* Ottawa: Bhakti Press, 1983.

Cameron, Dorothy. *Symbols of Birth and Death in the Neolithic Era.* London: Kenyan-Deane Ltd., 1981.

Casteneda, Carlos. *A Separate Reality.* New York: Pocket Books, 1971.

Chetwynd, Thomas. *A Dictionary of Symbols.* St. Albans, UK: Granada Press, 1982.

Crow, W. B. *The Arcana of Symbolism.* London: Aquarian Press, 1970.

Cunningham, Scott. *The Complete Book of Incense, Oils and Brews.* Minneapolis: Llewellyn Publications, 1989.

———. *Cunningham's Encyclopedia of Crystal, Gem and Metal Magic.* Minneapolis: Llewellyn Publishing, 1985.

———. *Earth, Air, Fire and Water: More Techniques of Natural Magic.* Minneapolis: Llewellyn Publications, 1991.

————. *Magickal Herbalism.* Minneapolis: Llewellyn Publications, 1982, 1983.

————. *Wicca, A Guide For The Solitary Practitioner.* Minneapolis: Llewellyn Publishing, 1988.

Curtis, Edward S. *The North American Indian,* vol. 1–17. New York: Johnson Reprint Corp., 1970.

Denig, Edwin. *Five Indian Tribes of the Upper Missouri.* Norman: University of Oklahoma Press, 1961.

Ebin, Victoria. *The Body Decorated.* London: Thames Hudson, 1979.

Eisler, Riane. *The Chalice and the Blade.* San Francisco: Harper & Row, 1987.

Eliade, Mircea. *Rites and Symbols of Initiation.* New York: Harper Collins, 1987.

————. *The Sacred and the Profane.* Chicago: University of Chicago Press, 1982.

Faris, James. *Nuba Personal Art.* Toronto: University of Toronto Press, 1972.

Farrar, Janet and Stewart. *Eight Sabbats for Witches.* Custer, WA: Phoenix Publishing, Inc., 1981.

————. *The Witches Way.* Custer, WA: Phoenix Publishing, Inc., 1984.

Fitch, Ed. *Magical Rites from the Crystal Well.* Minneapolis: Llewellyn Publishing, 1984.

Fellowes, C. H. *The Tattoo Book.* Princeton: The Pyne Press, 1983.

Galadriel. *The Magick of Incenses & Oils.* Atlanta: Grove of the Unicorn, 1976.

Gawain, Shakti. *Creative Visualization.* San Rafael: New World Library, 1978.

Gimbutas, Marija. *Goddesses and Gods of Old Europe.* Berkeley: University of California Press, 1982.

————. *Language of the Goddess.* New York: Harper & Row, 1989.

————. "The Beginning of the Bronze Age in Europe and the Europeans: 3500–2500," *Journal of Indo-European Studies,* no. 1.

————. "Vulvas, Breasts and Buttocks of the Goddess Creatress: Commentary on the Origins of Art," *The Shape of the Past: Studies in Honor of Franklin D. Murphy, Buccellati & Sperone.* Los Angeles: University of California Press, 1981.

Haldane, Suzanne. *Painting Faces.* New York: E. P. Dutton, 1988.

Harner, Michael. *The Way of the Shaman*. New York: Bantam Books, 1982.

Hawkes, Jacquetta. *Dawn of the Gods: Minoan and Mycenaean Origins of Greece*. New York: Rainbird Publishing, 1985.

Heavenly Fragrances. P.O. Box 951, Old Bridge, NJ, 08857.

Inman, Thomas. *Ancient Pagan and Modern Christian Symbols*. Kennebunkport, ME: Longwood Press, 1979.

Johnson, Buffy. *Lady of the Beasts*. San Francisco: Harper & Row, 1988.

Koch, Rudolf. *The Book of Signs*. New York: Dover Publications Inc., 1955.

Kunz, George F. *The Curious Lore of Precious Stones*. New York: Citadel, 1978.

Lowie, Robert H. *The Crow Indians*. New York: Holt, Rinehart and Winston, 1978.

Marshack, Alexander. "The Art and Symbols of Ice Age Man," *Human Nature*. September, 1978.

McQueen, Neil. "The Sacred in Art—The Painted Face and Body." Unpublished.

Medici, Marina. *Good Magic*. New York: Prentice Hall Press, 1988.

Mellaart, James. *Catal Huyuk*. New York: McGraw-Hill, 1967.

———. *Excavations at Hacilar*. Edinburgh: University of Edinburgh, 1970.

Miller, Richard A. *The Magical & Ritual Use of Aphrodisiacs*. New York: Destiny Books, 1986.

———. *The Magical & Ritual Use of Herbs*. New York: Destiny Books, 1983.

Nuttall, Zelia. (translation and commentary) *The Book of the Life of the Ancient Mexicans*. Berkeley: University of California Press, 1983.

Paulsen, Kathryn. *Witches' Potions and Spells*. Mt. Vernon, NY: Peter Pauper Press, 1987.

Pritchard, James. *The Ancient Near East in Pictures*. Princeton: Princeton University Press, 1954.

———. *Palestinian Figurines in Relation to Certain Goddesses Known Through Literature*. New Haven, CT: American Oriental Series, 1943.

Riefenstahl, Leni. *The Last of the Nuba*. New York: Harper & Row, 1974.

‡ ⊠ △ ◊ ⸸ □ Ν ⸸ ⸸ ▽ ⬙ Ϸ ⬠ ⋏ Γ Ϙ Ϸ ⊞ ⍊ △

——. *The People of Kau.* New York: Harper & Row, 1976.

Rose, Jean. *Jean Rose's Modern Herbal.* New York: Pedigree, 1987.

——. *Jeanne Rose's Herbal Body Book.* New York: Grosset and Dunlop, 1976.

Simmons, Leo. *Sun Chief.* New Haven, CT: Yale University Press, 1942.

Slater, Herman. *The Magical Formulary,* vol. I. New York: Magickal Childe Press, 1982.

——. *Pagan Rituals III.* New York: Magickal Childe Press, 1989.

Smith, C. Ray. *The Theater Crafts Book of Make-up, Masks, and Wigs.* Emmaus, PA: Rodale Press, 1974.

Starhawk. *The Spiral Dance.* 2nd ed. Revised and updated. San Francisco: Harper & Row, 1979.

Stark, Dr. Raymond. *The Book of Aphrodisiacs.* Toronto: Methuen Press, 1980.

Strathern, Anthony and Marilyn. *Self Decoration in Mt. Hagen.* Toronto: University of Toronto Press, 1971.

Stone, Merlin. *When God Was A Woman.* New York: Dial Press, 1976.

Thevoz, Michel. *The Painted Body.* New York: Skira Publishing, 1984.

Turner, Terence. "Tchikrin: A Central Brazilian Language of Bodily Adornment," *Natural History,* vol. 78., no. 8. October, 1969.

Ucko, Peter and Andree Rosenfeld. *Paleolithic Art.* New York: McGraw-Hill, 1967.

Ulydert, Mellie. *The Magic of Precious Stones.* Wellingborough, UK: Turnstone Press, 1982.

——. *Metal Magic—The Esoteric Properties and Uses of Metals.* Wellingborough, UK: Turnstone Press, 1980.

Vinci, Leo. *Incense—Its Ritual Significance, Use and Preparation.* Wellingborough, UK: Aquarian Press, 1980.

Vlahos, Olivia. *Body—The Ultimate Symbol, Meanings of the Human Body Through Time and Place.* New York: Lippincott, 1979.

Weinstein, Marion. *Positive Magic: Occult Self-Help.* Revised ed. Custer, WA: Phoenix Publishing, Inc., 1981.

Wolkstein, Diane and Samuel N. Kramer. *Inanna: Queen of Heaven and Earth.* New York: Harper & Row, 1983.

Appendix

The colors of Catal Huyuk, 6500–5750 BCE. from *Catal Huyuk,* by James Mellaart:

- red, brownish red, orange, yellow, and brown; all made from ocher
- an iron oxide red from hematite
- an iron ore dark red from cinnabar, a mercury oxide green from malachite
- a copper ore blue from azurite
- a copper ore mauve and purple from manganese gray from galena
- a lead ore white, cream, and buff, all from clays, black from soot, pink and pinkish red from unknown sources

Red, the indicator of life, is the most common house color, especially common above the household graves.

Black, the color of death to these ancient peoples, was found beneath the vulture figures and thus was the compliment of red in a society where life and death were viewed as equal states of existence.

When found, figures had no specific colors set aside for each sex. For example, women can be found in either red or white, while men, so far, are always found colored red with black hair.

Oddly enough, while bulls are found in both red and black, realistic colors aside from their symbolism for life and death, cows are found only in blue. Blue, with the exception of illustrating cows (the meaning of which is currently unknown) has, to date, been found in only one building where it, along with green (meaning also unknown), was applied to skeletons.